Average monthly temp
Average monthly rainfall

D0539213

PERTH AUSTRALIA	RIO DE JANEIRO BRAZIL	SYDNEY AUSTRALIA		U.K. ...ENT MONTH	MONTH
74°F – 23.5°C	78°F – 26°C	71°F – 22°C	64°F – 18°C	64°F – 18°C	JUL
0.3in – 7.6mm	4.9in – 12.7cm	3.5in – 8.9cm	0.1in – 2.8mm	2.0in – 51mm	
74°F – 23.5°C	79°F – 26.5°C	71°F – 22°C	64°F – 18°C	63°F – 17.5°C	AUG
0.4in – 10mm	4.8in – 12.3cm	4.0in – 10cm	0.1in – 2.7mm	2.2in – 56mm	
71°F – 22°C	77°F – 25°C	69°F – 20.5°C	62°F – 17°C	59°F – 15°C	SEP
0.8in – 20mm	5.1in – 13cm	5.0in – 13cm	0.3in – 7.6mm	1.8in – 46mm	
66°F – 19°C	74°F – 23.5°C	64°F – 18°C	59°F – 15°C	51°F – 10.5°C	OCT
1.7in – 43mm	4.2in – 11cm	5.3in – 13.5cm	0.6in – 15mm	2.3in – 58mm	
61°F – 16.5°C	71°F – 22°C	59°F – 15°C	56°F – 13.5°C	44°F – 7°C	NOV
5.1in – 13cm	3.1in – 8cm	5.0in – 13cm	4.1in – 10.5cm	2.5in – 63mm	
57°F – 14°C	70°F – 21°C	54°F – 12.5°C	54°F – 12.5°C	40°F – 4.5°C	DEC
7.1in – 18cm	2.1in – 54mm	4.6in – 10cm	5.9in – 15cm	2.0in – 52mm	
55°F – 13°C	69°F – 20.5°C	53°F – 12°C	53°F – 12°C	39°F – 4°C	JAN
6.7in – 17cm	1.6in – 41mm	4.6in – 12cm	3.9in – 10cm	2.0in – 52mm	
56°F – 13.5°C	70°F – 21°C	55°F – 13°C	54°F – 12.5°C	40°F – 4.5°C	FEB
5.7in – 14.5cm	1.7in – 45mm	3.0in – 8cm	2.9in – 7.3cm	1.5in – 38mm	
58°F – 14.5°C	70°F – 21°C	59°F – 15°C	55°F – 13°C	44°F – 7°C	MAR
3.4in – 8.6cm	2.6in – 66mm	2.9in – 74mm	1.3in – 33mm	1.4in – 36mm	
61°F – 16.5°C	71°F – 22°C	63°F – 17.5°C	57°F – 14°C	48°F – 9°C	APR
2.2in – 56mm	3.1in – 8cm	2.8in – 71mm	0.4in – 10mm	1.8in – 46mm	
66°F – 19°C	73°F – 23°C	67°F – 19.5°C	60°F – 16°C	54°F – 12.5°C	MAY
0.8in – 20cm	4.1in – 10.5cm	2.9in – 73mm	0.2in – 5mm	1.8in – 46mm	
71°F – 22°C	76°F – 24.5°C	67°F – 19.5°C	62°F – 17°C	60°F – 16°C	JUN
0.5in – 12mm	5.4in – 14cm	2.9in – 74mm	0.2in – 5mm	1.6in – 41mm	

See back end-papers for Northern Hemisphere chart.

BONSAI

The Collingridge Handbook of

BONSAI

ANNE SWINTON

With a preface by
Anthony Huxley

Photographs by
Dick Robinson
and line drawings by
Ron Hayward

COLLINGRIDGE

Acknowledgements

First I must thank Dick Robinson for his superb photography throughout this book, which has added so much to its value. Secondly, Anthony Huxley for writing the preface, which reflects his understanding of bonsai as a craft, a science and an art form. He has also provided the unique selection of photographs on pages 18 and 19 of bonsai specimens encountered during his visit to China in the autumn of 1981.

To Anne Haw my gratitude for spending countless hours typing the manuscript, proof reading and much else, and to my fellow director in our bonsai business, Tony Sweeney, my thanks for his support.

I am grateful to Murphy Chemical Ltd. for permission to reproduce the photographs of azalea gall and coral spot; and the Ministry of Agriculture, Fisheries and Food for that of crown gall. I must also thank the publishers of the following books for permission to make quotations, as credited on the appropriate pages: Penguin Books, Routledge and Kegan Paul Ltd., and Wildwood House.

A.S.

Published by Collingridge Books
an imprint of Newnes Books
a division of The Hamlyn Publishing Group Limited
84–88 The Centre, Feltham, Middlesex, TW13 4BH
and distributed for them by
The Hamlyn Publishing Group Limited
Rushden, Northants, England

First published 1982
Third impression 1983

ISBN 0 600 36816 5

Printed in Great Britain by
Hazell Watson & Viney Limited,
Member of the BPCC Group,
Aylesbury, Bucks

CONTENTS

COLOUR PLATES

PREFACE

Anthony Huxley, M.A., V.M.H.

The miniature has exercised its fascination since man first practised any kind of art in the form of tiny stone or bone carvings and clay statuettes. Such miniatures were portable, like amulets; and indeed many such early works of art were without doubt magical in intent.

In the same way the plant miniature, in metaphysical terms, encapsulates magical powers and natural energy, according to the principles of the Taoist religion, especially if contorted and shaped by adverse conditions. This is the basic origin of the bonsai tree.

There are those who regard bonsai as grotesque, distortions, even mutilations. Certainly there have been periods, especially in China, when bonsai trees were deliberately grotesque; equally some modern commercial "bonsai" – they do not deserve the name – are the result of substantial mutilation. At their best, however, bonsai trees or tree groups appear to be scaled-down versions of natural growth, shaped in accordance with long tradition, undoubted works of art created over decades if not centuries of work.

This is one of the messages of this book. There are no real-short-cuts to creating a worthwhile bonsai tree. Initial training calls for patience combined with an eye for the potential of each immature specimen, which in the course of time becomes intuitive. In her work Anne Swinton has developed this faculty to a remarkable degree, making quick decisions about pruning and training. This is a desirable attribute since, as a professional grower, she is processing trees in considerable numbers.

Processing may seem an ugly word to use, but remember that any work of art needs initial preparation – like canvas for painting or the rough-hewn block of material for sculpture. The early stages of bonsai culture are certainly processes, the mechanics of which can look quite artificial for a time. But they must be based on a deep understanding of the plant's reactions to trimming, bending or pinching.

The fact that Anne Swinton is a professional grower does not make her in any way unaware that the amateur of bonsai can, in the first place, achieve his or her ends from seeds, cuttings or wild seedlings without ever buying even partly formed trees, and with a minimum of simple household tools. In the second place, she realises that, as in most forms of art which amateurs may try, they are, initially at least, unlikely to achieve masterpieces but will enjoy the process of creating something pleasing, living and unique to themselves; nor do they need to steep themselves in the religious origins, interesting as they are.

One of the pleasures of this book is an account of the many trees which lend themselves to the technique, and while describing the formation and various possible final forms of bonsai Anne Swinton quietly dispenses the essential – and almost inexpressible – feeling of what makes a good specimen. In particular, this is never a matter of size. Few of us can hope to own really large, ancient specimens: some commercial growers manipulate young trees to appear as such, but apart from being less likely to survive to great ages, such specimens seldom possess real quality.

The author's own trees reflect true quality and illustrations of them, with long descriptive captions, are an integral part of this book. I am specially pleased that all these were photographed by my colleague Dick Robinson (using, as a matter of technical interest, a Rollei SL66 camera). While I am glad to have contributed the pictures of Chinese pen-jing I regret that circumstances made it impossible to do better technically. At least they are, as far as I know, the first set of such photographs to appear in a book published in this country. Apart from their intrinsic interest, they also serve to remind us that the dwarfed tree originated in China and continues to be widely grown there.

This matter of bonsai's origin is one aspect of the historical perspective into which Anne Swinton places the subject, the other, equally important, being Zen Buddhism. As she writes, "the slow cultivation of the bonsai and the patience necessary for nurturing it . . . can together be a form of meditation. . . In growing it the individual can be led to a far greater appreciation of the process of life."

At whatever level it is approached, bonsai culture is a fascinating pastime, and this extremely informative book will help any one to enjoy it to the full.

CHAPTER ONE

THE HISTORICAL BACKGROUND

The art of training trees in small containers has been practised for many centuries. Although there are contemporary records of potted trees in many countries, both in the East and in Europe, credit for the development of this skill into the art-form known as bonsai must lie with the Japanese.

BONSAI IN CHINA

In China, dwarfed trees in pots have been cultivated for over one thousand years. The practice probably stemmed from the principles of Taoism, the followers of which believed that the presentation of certain natural phenomena, such as mountains or trees in miniature, allowed them to focus on the magical properties present and obtain some of these powers. The greater the reduction in size, the higher the concentration of magic was believed to be.

The Taoists believed that a contorted, gnarled shape represented the grotesquely twisted bodies of those who wished to enter the "other world" (the world beyond mortality). Those who achieved immortality would have great age, be twisted and distorted far from the normal shape, and appear shrunken and withered.

As would be expected in a country of such varied topography, regional variations in the style of potted trees became evident as their popularity grew. During the Ming and Ch'ing dynasties (1368–1644 and 1644–1911, respectively), the potted trees reflected, to an extent, the surrounding countryside and local traditions. In the Lake district, the "flat top" style contrasted with the "Pagoda" style of the Yangchow region. Trees were receiving training to create these effects, rather than collectors relying solely on naturally dwarfed trees to provide their material. A number of 12th and 13th century paintings illustrate potted trees, notably Peeping at the Bath attributed to Chang Tse-tuan, and The Reclining Pine by Li Shih-hsing, the latter of especial interest as it is a picture of a pine tree in a pot. Why this is so will become clear later.

At the beginning of the 20th century, Cantonese growers began training trees by a "grow and clip" method. This produced trees of an ancient and, to Western eyes, gnarled appearance, reminiscent of Chinese brush paintings. This school of bonsai tree training is known as the "Lingnan" school and has, by and large, superseded more ancient methods of training trees, now only continued in certain centres of garden art, such as Suchow.

A group of modern, Chinese-trained bonsai exhibited by the Chinese National Nature Produce Corporation at the 1980 Chelsea Flower Show.

BONSAI IN JAPAN

The history of bonsai in Japan does not cover quite such a long period. The first authentic Japanese record of bonsai is in 1309 on a picture scroll by Takakane Takashina, known as Kasugagongen-genki. Other written or painted records of similar date indicate that bonsai were known and appreciated by the aristocracy during the Kamakura period (1180–1333), when trees in specially-made ceramic containers were placed near the house or on the verandah for display. The training or styling of larger trees was also practised at this time, coinciding with a considerable and growing interest in landscaping and gardens. However, bonsai were to become better known during the two and a half centuries of the Muro machi period. A famous Noh play *Hachi-no-ki (Trees in Pots)*, written by Seami (1363–1444), dwelt on the significance of three bonsai, a pine, a cherry and an apricot to their owner, Tsuneyo, a poor yeoman, who nevertheless burnt them one snowy night to warm an unexpected guest. The guest, in appearance a priest, was in fact the retired Regent of the Kamakura Shogunate, Tokiyori.

Naturally dwarfed trees were collected and potted but it was only towards the end of the period that the idea of improving the shape of these wild trees began to develop. Already, younger trees were being trained in a style known as "tako" to satisfy the demands of the increasingly powerful merchant classes who were becoming interested in the arts. To cater for their needs many "tako" styled trees were commercially produced, their trunks shaped by tying with hemp into coils, equally spaced and decreasing in size to give an overall pyramidal shape and the effect of a gnarled, twisted tree.

The Tokugawa period (1603–1867) which followed was a period of peace under a feudal government. Development of the arts became an important preoccupation and both bonsai and other Japanese horticultural skills were to reach high levels of achievement towards its end. Not only were there great steps forward in the development of ornamental garden plants but also the skills and techniques associated with gardening and landscape gardening. In particular, bonsai benefited from the heightened interest in the Southern school of painting and the development of literati bonsai (see page 83). For a while, grotesquely distorted trees were considered as good bonsai but this tendency was, fortunately, short-lived.

By the early eighteenth century, bonsai in many of the styles seen today were present in the nursery of Ibei Ito, a noted nurseryman and author. An illustration of the nursery by Kiyoharu shows trees of cascading, weeping, twin-truck and other forms but no "tako" trained trees. The containers used for bonsai were, up to and beyond this time, of a greater depth than those in use today. Not until the early nineteenth century, in *Kinsei-jufu*, published in 1830, is there mention of shallower pots of a wider range of shapes.

In 1867 the feudal government fell and Japan entered a more modern world. Ideas developed at great speed as horizons broadened and bonsai benefited from this momentum. "Natural" bonsai were eagerly collected from the mountains by professional collectors. These were then developed skilfully and trained to enhance their beauty. Many nurseries were set up to train young trees to assume the shapes of the wild ones, so satisfying the demands of a liberated society to enjoy the pleasures formerly reserved for the aristocrats and the wealthy. "Tako" style trees were no longer trained, but the feeling this style of training evoked has been retained in the "horai" style by the people of the village of Honai in Echigo province (North-west Japan) for the training of Japanese white pine, *Pinus parviflora*. The glaucous, short-needled form known as shimofuri is grafted in great numbers on to black pine *(Pinus thunbergii)* stocks before being trained by coiling them round pegs of mulberry wood and fastening with rice straw. The trees are grown in fields, lifted each year for training, then replanted, producing a sizeable "trained" bonsai in some six or seven years.

UNDERSTANDING BONSAI

By the turn of the century, bonsai were being regularly exported, the first exhibition of Japanese plants being staged in London in 1909. This created considerable interest amongst an Edwardian public which was more accustomed to gardening on the grand scale, but it is mainly in the past 20 years that an increasingly well-informed public has become more involved in the art.

As with other Oriental arts, however, certain misconceptions have always existed in the West. For many years the belief was widely held that bonsai were special Japanese trees which grew in an unusual and attractive way because of their genetic make-up, that they were in fact mystical dwarf varieties. For other people the cultivation of bonsai has sometimes even been associated with Oriental practices such as foot-binding in China – a practice which, for the Chinese, had a quite different significance from what might be supposed – but generally the arts in Japan, with their close religious associations, have enjoyed a high degree of respect, even though they have not always been above criticism.

As long ago as the 13th century, the satirical author Kenko Yoshido wrote "To appreciate and find pleasure in curiously curved, potted trees is to love deformity." He was talking about the fashion increasingly prevalent among the upper classes at that time for growing bonsai, though he may also have been commenting on the quality of trees commercially produced to satisfy this demand. However, such a misconception is understandable. Even today in Japan, there is some disagreement between purists and others as to what exactly constitutes a bonsai. Traditionally, trees that had been dwarfed or stunted by nature and undernourished were used. Struggling in poor soil and adverse conditions, they were collected by bonsai growers as their starting point, and it could take up to 50 years of meticulous and patient training of one of them to achieve a miniature tree that could be considered by its owner to approach perfection. This protracted method of cultivation of the traditionalists has largely given way in more recent years to the modern method of raising bonsai from cuttings or seeds, and nowadays it is possible to establish one within a much shorter period of time. Depending on its style of training, an immature bonsai of five years may display enough charm to be exhibited alongside mature specimens. However, it is important to emphasise that a bonsai, although small in stature, should be healthy and growing vigorously, being supplied with nourishment adequate for its top growth. A tree that is starving or lacking in vigour is not a good one.

To qualify as a bonsai the finshed product will usually be tree-like in appearance. There are exceptions, however, and in Japan at least certain plants such as chrysanthemums, grasses and rushes are trained for display as bonsai. Again, it is possible to have a "miniature of a miniature", which is the case with mame or miniature bonsai. These are raised in the same way as other bonsai from ordinary, or in certain circumstances dwarf, varieties (see Chapter 3). They provide a challenge to the grower in that, even though much smaller than the usual bonsai, they still retain the appearance of a tree, and do not simply look like tiny plants. They are so small that several may be accommodated in the space taken up by a window box, and a number of mame bonsai displayed together can give quite a charming effect.

THE INFLUENCE OF ZEN BUDDHISM

Every bonsai should be trained with an eye for the proportion and harmony of its component parts. At first sight some styles of training may seem to be

LEFT: Pinus parviflora, *trained in the Horai style.* RIGHT: *A 14-year-old English elm* (Ulmus procera), *6in (15cm) high. It was originally a wild seedling.*

contrived and difficult for the western mind to appreciate. The art of bonsai, however, is not meant to be a mere reproduction of nature. Rather, it aims to symbolise or encapsulate nature in a perfect miniature tree, which may be grown by itself in a carefully selected container, with other trees, or clasped round a stone, the whole achieving a strikingly spontaneous and apparently natural appearance.

Buddhism reached Japan via China as early as the 6th century AD and was transmuted into the uniquely Japanese form that we know as Zen. It was largely through the work of Dr Daisetz Suzuki, beginning with a paper written for the Journal of the Pali Society of London in 1908, that Zen was introduced to the West, where it has been taken up at various times, especially in America, as something of a cult. The difficulty for most Westerners in understanding Zen is that it is more a way of life than a formal religion; it has no fixed laws or dogmas, and often expresses itself in abrupt and seemingly insoluble paradoxes or riddles, known as "koans". Great stress is laid upon self-discipline, contemplation and pre-conceived ideas. Its appeal to the Westerner lies in its apparent simplicity, its tolerance and atmosphere of freedom, and in the peace of mind to be gained from the practice of meditation.

The Japanese attitude to art and to nature differs quite substantially from the Western viewpoint, and it is perhaps not possible to appreciate to the full such activities as bonsai growing without some understanding of the principles of Zen Buddhism. Dr Suzuki has said that "Art is studied in Japan

Carpinus betulus, *found in an area of landslides with a strangely twisted trunk. The branches have been developed in the semi-cascade style.*

not only for Art's sake but for spiritual enlightenment".[1] This is the basis for the whole Japanese approach to the study of such things as painting, poetry, flower arrangement and gardening, and it is extended to encompass such diverse and apparently unrelated activities as the practice of Judo, and the formal tea ceremony, to mention but two. In this way Zen Buddhism permeates every aspect of Japanese culture.

Zen perceives life as a unity of which man, art and nature form harmonious and inseparable parts. Through this understanding of the unity of all things, we can apprehend something of life's mystery, and see the eternal in even the smallest manifestation of nature, or the simplest work of art. This concept is not entirely alien to the Western mind. The mystical poet William Blake (1757–1827) expressed very much the same idea, when he wrote in his *Auguries of Innocence* of the ability "To see a World in a Grain of Sand, And a Heaven in a Wild Flower . . . . . . "

In the same way the bonsai tree stands for something much larger than itself; in fact, the slow cultivation of the bosai and the patience necessary for nurturing it through its various stages of growth can together be a kind of meditation. There need be no sense of frustration in the knowledge that it will continue to live and develop long after its first owner has died. In

[1]From the introduction to *Zen in the Art of Flower Arrangement*, by G. L. Herrigel (translated from the German by R. F. C. Hull), Routledge and Keegan Paul.

growing it the individual can be led to a far deeper appreciation of the process of life – a kind of oneness with nature and with the universe – that cannot be achieved merely by looking at nature from a sentimental standpoint.

Chinese Taoist writings stress the importance of an attitude of respect towards the universe. Lao Tsu, in the *Tao Te Ching*[2] of the 6th century BC, states that, "When men lack a sense of awe, there will be disaster". We find the same thought running through the writings of Basho, the 17th century Japanese Haiku poet. On one of his journeys he records that he saw a huge pine tree, probably over one thousand years old, and he wrote, "As I stood in front of this tree, I felt a strange sense of awe and respect, for, though the tree itself was a cold senseless object it had survived the punishment of an axe for so many years under the divine protection of Buddha."[3] Basho, demonstrating his almost spiritual appreciation of nature, also warns against a too-subjective approach, when he says, "Go to the pine if you want to learn about the pine, or to the bamboo if you want to learn about the bamboo. And in doing so, you must leave your subjective preoccupation with yourself. Otherwise you impose yourself on the subject and do not learn."[4]

Although this advice was concerned with poetry, the lesson has obvious relevance for all forms of artistic expression when he continues: "Your poetry issues of its own accord when you and the object have become one – when you have plunged deep enough into the object to see something like a hidden glimmering there. However well-phrased your poetry may be, if your feeling is not natural – if the object and yourself are separate – then your poetry is not true poetry but merely your subjective counterfeit."[5]

Bonsai with their varying sizes can either be so small as to be highly portable or so large that they can be regarded as containerised, trained trees. It is in this range of stature that one can identify both the influence of the landscaping skills of garden design and the styles favoured for flower arrangements.

As we have seen, Japanese gardening and flower arranging had their origins with the Zen masters. The monastic life adopted these disciplines as an aid to enlightenment, and in so doing set a spiritual seal on its future development amongst the laity. The orderly rhythm of the monk's life and the time available, enabled the right kind of knowledge to be developed to a high degree and to be handed down to successive generations. The master-pupil relationship in Japan has traditionally been an important one, every discipline involving the same atmosphere of respect and reverence for learning. According to this tradition the ideal way of acquiring an understanding of bonsai is to learn from a teacher through lessons and not through the medium of the written word. The pupil's learning process would involve close supervision, the teacher (sensei) demanding high standards. Learning

---

[2]*Tao Te Ching* – Lao Tsu (translated by Gia-fu Feng and Jane English) Wildwood House.

[3,4 and 5]*The Narrow Road to the Deep North and Other Travel Sketches*, by Basho, (translated by Nobuyuki Yuasa), Penguin Classics, copyright © Nobuyuki Yuasa, 1966.

was associated with the maintenance of spiritual values and the pupil was in a special position for acquiring knowledge of, not only the chosen discipline, but also of spiritual growth. There was at all times an interaction between the imparting of knowledge and the parallel development of personal qualities as a human being. The sensei's role was not therefore confined to instruction, but in addition to his teaching, he offered a paternalistic and almost priestly guidance.

This type of relationship is not unique to the East as something rather similar was prevalent during the Renaissance in Europe. Young artists lived with the great masters for many years, learning their skills with great thoroughness. Initially their responsibilities were confined to menial tasks such as mixing paints, cleaning brushes and preparing canvasses, but as their awareness grew, they became involved with the painting of less important areas of the masters' works before finally becoming artists in their own right. Due to this very gradual acquisition of knowledge even early works of these artists show a degree of sympathy with their subject matter and a skill in execution rarely seen in naturally talented but less schooled painters. To a more limited extent, the tradition has continued to the present day in Europe amongst craft-workers, it being almost essential to learn many of the skills combining artistry and manual dexterity from one who is practised in the art.

BONSAI IN CHINA TODAY

With the gradual improvement in access to parts of China for the Western visitor, interest in Chinese bonsai (known to the Chinese as pen-jing or artistic trees in pots) is being greatly increased. Though their styles and methods of training have changed somewhat over the years, they remain as yet little influenced by Japanese bonsai traditions and as a result offer to the enthusiast a new opportunity to study trees which are the product of many centuries of accumulated skills.

There are a few collections of very fine old bonsai in China, such as those in the historic gardens in Suchow, where ancient and often extremely large potted trees may be seen. And again, smaller, younger bonsai are a normal decorative feature in many hotels, some of these having their own nurseries, producing bonsai along with shrubs and bulbs. Occasionally a few trees may be available for purchase. Bonsai are also frequently displayed in public places, notably railway stations, and small trees may be placed for decorative purposes on the tables of railway compartments.

As one would expect in a country with such a wide range of trees as China, the plants selected for training are very diverse, and include such little-known species as *Sageretia theesans, Murraya paniculata* and *Serissa foetida* (tree of a thousand stars), as well as the more usually seen *Ulmus, Acer, Pinus* and so on. These are planted as individual specimens or in a group, often of mixed species and usually in conjunction with rocks. The Chinese regard for rocks will be already known to those who have studied Chinese landscape gardening, and sometimes bonsai or other small trees may be

A group of small and mame bonsai, including Cotoneaster horizontalis, Ulmus procera, *pyracantha,* Spiraea japonica *and parthenocissus.*

dispensed with altogether in favour of a landscape of rock on its own, displayed in a shallow tray.

Individual bonsai in China, both the older examples and those more recently grown and trained, differ significantly from the Japanese or Western examples. The initial visual impact of a bonsai is always influenced by its container, and in China the majority of containers used are deep and round. They are commonly of a reddish-brown, unglazed pottery or, for a few selected specimens, a glazed pot, probably antique, may be used.

The majority of the bonsai seen to date by visitors to China appear to differ substantially in shape from those of Japan. This is no doubt in part due to the far wider range of species cultivated, each of which offers its own problems in training, but is also influenced by the differing ideals of beauty and the different significance of bonsai to the peoples of the two countries. When comparing pines, for example, it becomes obvious that the Chinese emphasis is on producing a tree with a canopy-like crown of some size, whereas in the Japanese bonsai pine great importance is laid on the spread of the lower branches, a feature which is repeated in Japanese landscape gardening.

Sageretia theesans (which is not a form of plum, despite its popular Chinese name of sparrow-plum) is often seen in China trained with a relatively bare, straight trunk, from which grow branches each carrying a compact, tightly-controlled clump of foliage, the whole thing being reminiscent of topiary and in a similar style, in fact, to many trained trees in Thailand.

RIGHT: *A group of four* Pinus parviflora *(a number rarely used in Japan) in a typical Chinese room setting in the Hangchow Gallery.*

ABOVE: *An interesting planting of* Pinus parviflora *among rocks on a large stone tray. This is one of the biggest tray plantings seen by Anthony Huxley in China.*

LEFT: *Bonsai bamboo in an interesting and very Chinese setting in the exhibition gallery of Hangchow bonsai nursery.*

ABOVE: *The entrance to the Hangchow bonsai nursery. The moongate, flanked by specimens of* Pinus parviflora, *is at one and the same time restful and compelling.*
BELOW: *A large* Sageretia theesans *trained in the grow and clip style now much used in China, and flanked by cascade style trees on ornate pillars. In the foreground is a composition of rock, standing in water.*

Podocarpus is also sometimes used, and may be seen in various shapes, some having winding trunks. Others, clearly originating in the wild, have thick trunks ending rather abruptly with a few small branches, but the commonest are *Pinus parviflora*, various acers, *Pinus thunbergii* and some *Ginkgo*.

From the little information as yet available, it would appear that artistically-trained trees in pots are not a regular feature in Chinese homes, bulbs and succulents being more usual. This may, of course, relate to the cost of bonsai, but it may also be influenced by the great numbers of bonsai of all sorts which people can see elsewhere each day, and to the fact that many Chinese live in flats with no place for display outside. It remains to be seen whether the cultivation of bonsai stays confined to the small, specialist nurseries, as would appear to be the case at present, or whether it will become, as it has in Japan and the West, a hobby followed by many. As more and more literature on the Chinese bonsai becomes available it will be interesting to see whether enthusiasts in Western countries attempt to cultivate some of the Chinese kinds alongside their own and Japanese examples.

WESTERN BONSAI TODAY

The heritage of bonsai offers to the modern world a hobby that can provide many spheres of interest. To the western horticulturist it can offer contact with Japanese culture and oriental art. To the artist who is looking for a new medium of expression it is a challenge, in that it involves an exacting application of horticultural skills. Many Western countries have adopted Japanese arts and sports and achieved a high level of excellence in the last 20 to 30 years. With an increase in leisure time, this trend can be expected to continue. Alongside a revival of interest in traditional Western crafts, the next few decades can provide a period when Western culture may make an original contribution to aspects of oriental culture such as bonsai.

CHAPTER TWO

FORMING
A COLLECTION

For those who are interested in plants, gardens, and in particular trees, the idea of growing bonsai may offer a new and rather different approach to the traditional British hobby of gardening. With the modern rush of everyday living the tranquility of a bonsai might seem more attractive than does backbreaking digging or regular lawn mowing. For the disabled, the cultivation of bonsai offers a way of gardening while sitting down and without the problems of, for instance, moving large quantities of soil or of planting a herbaceous border. Again, many people do not have gardens at all but live in flats without even having a balcony. All of these, young and old, rich and poor, can learn the art of raising and training bonsai and gain a richly rewarding hobby. Young children, perhaps set a task in a nature study class to grow a tree from an acorn, rapidly develop an interest in the idea of making the young oak a pretty shape. From such a small beginning can develop a life-long affection for trees of all sizes.

There are many ways of starting a collection, three of which are currently very popular. These are as follows:

GROWING FROM SEED There are many people who like to feel that the results of their efforts are all their own work. For them, growing trees from seed is ideal, although surprise is frequently expressed at the small size of the seeds, which can be bought or else collected from native trees. Growing trees from seed is very cheap, intensely satisfying and surprisingly easy, even for the complete novice. Most tree seeds require stratification to break dormancy and commence germination. Stratification is the practice of over-wintering them, either out of doors or in a refrigerator, so giving them the "winter" they would have under natural circumstances. The needs of individual kinds differ somewhat, but many respond favourably to three to four weeks in a domestic refrigerator before planting. While in the refrigerator, they should be kept moist, and this is easily achieved with small quantities by mixing them with damp sand in an egg cup. Many tree seeds flourish with this treatment and if they are collected in the autumn and stored until winter, they can then be stratified and planted in time for the onset of spring. Among the commoner trees are beech and oak, but seeds from these two should be planted straight away after collection as they rapidly lose their viability when stored.

As seeds begin to germinate they should be regularly checked to ensure they do not become too wet or too dry. When two or three true leaves have

LEFT: *A five-year-old oak tree grown "for fun" from an acorn.* RIGHT: *The same tree photographed one week later, pruned and re-potted as a start to bonsai training.*

emerged, the seedlings can be transplanted for their training as bonsai to begin.

SEEDLINGS FROM THE WILD Young seedlings from the wild are an excellent starting ground for the impatient novice who, concerned about the time he might have to spend looking at a seed tray of compost, feels he would like to have something there to look at straight away. Many readily obtainable seedlings are suitable, and a search round even a small town garden could reveal enough suitable ones to start a far from modest collection. It is wise to dig up several small seedlings in case of losses due to inexperience, and to put them into flower pots, this being the first stage of their training. Once they are established the fun starts, and a great deal can be learnt in trying to train them. It is likely that one or two will begin to look attractive quite quickly, several will be only average, and an odd two or three will be destined to baffle their owners because of their particular size, shape or growth habit. If seedlings are growing on other peoples property, heed my words on p. 31.

CUTTINGS Many bonsai may be obtained by propagating from cuttings. Once rooted, these can be trained in the same way as a seedling tree. There are a number of advantages in growing from cuttings, one being the certainty that the young plant will have the same characteristics as the parent plant, i.e. leaf size, colour and growth habit. Another, especially relevant with plants grown for flowers or fruit, is the far shorter time one must wait before the young plants will flower for the first time.

The majority of people will, when they think of cuttings, have in mind a shoot or stem of a tree or shrub. This type of cutting is the sort most frequently taken but root cuttings and bud cuttings of certain plants will also grow and can be used to make plants for future bonsai training. Leaf cuttings, which are taken for the propagation of plants such as the African violet (*Saintpaulia*) and begonia, are rarely of use to the bonsai grower, but three sorts of stem cutting are commonly recognised, these being described as "soft", "semi-hardwood" and "hardwood".

SOFTWOOD CUTTINGS Softwood cuttings can be taken from outdoor trees and shrubs during June and July and are formed from non-flowering shoots of the current year's growth, firm but in no way woody. They should be up to about 4 in (10 cm) long and be severed with a sharp knife from the parent plant just below a leaf node, or pulled off at the point where they join a bigger stem, with a "heel" of older wood attached. The heel will need to be trimmed before the cutting is ready to insert into the rooting medium. Soft cuttings require warm, humid, conditions for rooting and the rooting medium will need to be kept at a temperature of about 60°F (16°C). A close, moist atmosphere diminishes the need for transpiration.

Commercially, such cuttings are rooted with the aid of mist equipment on heated, thermostatically controlled benching. The rooting medium is kept at a predetermined temperature, while the mist jets, controlled by a humidity-sensitive or a light-sensitive device give out a fine mist spray that cools the leaves and keeps the water content of the air high while not overwatering. This type of equipment is expensive to install and to run, but the amateur with only a few cuttings will get quite good results from using pots and trays standing over a source of heat and covered with a "tent" of polythene. People have differing ideas as to the ideal rooting medium but generally a mixture of peat and coarse sand or sharp grit is considered most suitable. Vermiculite and polystyrene granules are frequently substituted for grit, these having the advantages of lightness and cleanness.

When cuttings have been taken, they should be prepared for planting as quickly as possible. One or two lower leaves may be removed to give a clean stem to insert into the rooting medium and reduce moisture losses by transpiration but as many as possible should be left to manufacture the food the new plant needs and to ensure root growth. Rooting may be helped if cuttings are dipped in a proprietary hormone rooting powder before insertion, this being used according to the manufacturer's instructions. Finally, the cuttings are inserted into the rooting medium for about one-third of their length. Use a dibber to make holes for them (an old ball-point pen or chopstick makes an excellent tool for this job) and space them out sufficiently to prevent the foliage of adjacent cuttings touching each other.

As soon as the cuttings have rooted, they should be potted up (the rooting medium has no food value) and hardened off. If, for some reason, the procedure has to be delayed, the plants should be fed with a little liquid fertiliser. The growing-on compost should consist of loam, leaf mould and sharp sand (equal parts by volume).

The earlier softwood cuttings are rooted, the better established will be the

A

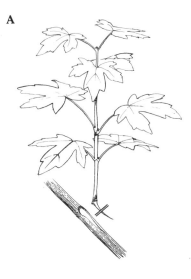

B

C

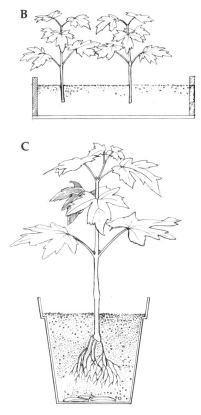

A. *A cutting taken with a heel of older wood attached.* **B.** *Cuttings prepared and inserted in the rooting medium.* **C.** *A rooted cutting potted up in a flower pot ready for preliminary bonsai training.*

resulting plants before the arrival of autumn prevents further growth. It is an advantage if the stock plant, from which cuttings will be taken, can be brought into the greenhouse early in spring. This will encourage it to start growing much sooner than if it is left in the open.

SEMI-HARDWOOD CUTTINGS Semi-hardwood cuttings are, as their name suggests, firmer than softwood ones but less mature than hardwood. These are generally taken from July to September, and are most successfully rooted in the protected environment of a cold frame. They generally take longer to root than softwood cuttings and should therefore be larger, about 6 in (15 cm.) long if possible, though conifer cuttings may be about 4 in (10 cm.), and they should be removed from the parent plant with a heel of older wood attached. Any very young growth at the top of the shoot should be removed and the cuttings, after the heels are trimmed and the lower leaves removed, should be inserted up to half their length in pots or boxes containing a suitable rooting medium. This generally consists of equal parts, by volume, of peat and propagating grit or coarse sand. The cold frame lights should remain closed to maintain humidity and the cuttings will require spraying over with clear water at least once a day. During sunny periods partial shading can be provided by using sackcloth or plastic netting especially made for the purpose.

The following spring, the rooted cuttings may be planted out in rows in the open ground or be potted up. Those which have formed a callus at their base but have formed no roots should be discarded, unless they are of rare species or varieties or are otherwise hard to obtain. Under these circumstances a little of the callus may be pared away and the cuttings reinserted into a propagating medium with a little bottom heat. They may then be persuaded to root.

HARDWOOD CUTTINGS Hardwood cuttings are the easiest to deal with, being taken during the late autumn and winter months when deciduous trees and shrubs are dormant. Long cuttings – 6 to 15 in (15 to 38 cm) depending on variety – are taken, either with a heel or cut beneath a leaf node, and they should be of completely ripe wood.

A v-shaped trench should be dug in good fertile soil in a sheltered, well-drained part of the garden and 1 in (2.5 cm) of sand sprinkled in the bottom. The cuttings should be laid against one side of the trench with their bases resting on the sand. Soil should then be pushed back into the trench and firmed thoroughly. If this firming is neglected frosts could loosen the cuttings. They are best left in the ground for a year before transplanting or re-potting.

LEAF-BUD CUTTINGS Leaf-bud cuttings are another form of propagation successful with certain types of plant. They require similar conditions to softwood cuttings and are taken during the summer. A section of stem is taken which includes one leaf. This section may be only a "half moon" cut from the stem as long as it includes the leaf, and the cutting should be inserted in the rooting medium so that only the leaf is showing. This method

A. A leaf bud cutting removed from a stem. B. A leaf bud cutting taken with a small length of stem attached.

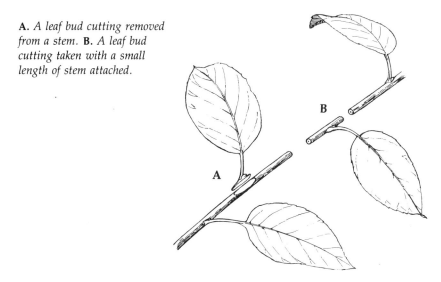

of propagation may be used when there is a shortage of propagating material or if it particularly suits a certain kind of plant. *Camellia japonica* is readily increased by this method.

ROOT CUTTINGS Root cuttings can be taken from those trees which form adventitious buds on their roots. Such trees include poplars, elms and quinces. Selected roots are removed in winter and should be cut straight across at the top end and trimmed with a sloping cut at the other end. These, which can be of variable length, 2 to 3 in (5 to 8 cm) or more in some cases, should then be inserted the correct way up in pots containing a rooting medium of equal parts by volume of peat, coarse grit and loam. They should be covered with ½ in (1 cm) of sand and pots may be left outside or in a cold frame during the winter. In spring, shoots will develop from the roots, at which stage the young plants so obtained may be potted on for future use.

Root cuttings will also produce shoots when sections of root are buried horizontally in the rooting medium. This is advantageous to the bonsai grower who wishes to grow trees intended for training in the raft style (see p. 83).

BUYING PARTIALLY-TRAINED PLANTS Some would-be collectors feel happier if they have a partially-trained bonsai to guide them. If they are fortunate enought to buy one direct from one of the very few bonsai specialists in Britain they may also learn from them a considerable amount about its care and future training, but there are many ways in which a bonsai can be purchased other than from a specialist. However, plants from less reliable sources may or may not result in a good bonsai being obtained at a reasonable price.

RIGHT: *Prepared root cuttings, each with a flat top and sloping bottom, inserted in rooting medium.*

BELOW: *Root cutting planted horizontally. The shoots are trained as trunks of a root-connected bonsai.*

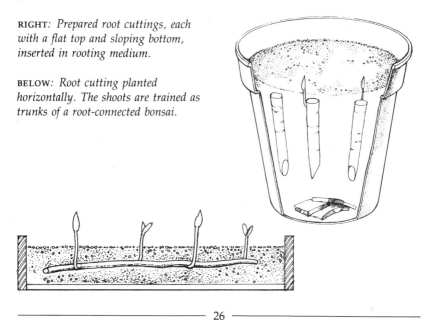

Advertisements appear frequently in the national press urging readers to purchase "young bonsai", at very low prices and suggesting the advantages of a ready-made garden of little trees, evergreen or deciduous, to be kept either indoors or outdoors. But one should bear in mind when seeing such advertisements that bonsai are, or should be, trained trees, and with present-day labour and land costs little in the way of training can have taken place for such offers to be made. The "little trees" referred to can be no more than uprooted seedlings; no more needs to be said.

Some florists' shops are now, in response to requests from their clients, stocking bonsai which can be examined before purchase. This is, of course, preferable, but just the same has a number of hidden disadvantages. The price is likely to be higher than the cost of a similar tree at a specialist nursery for one thing. However, as the convenience of visiting a local florist can far outweigh the cost and time taken to visit a specialist, who may be very many miles away, the purchaser may feel that this particular drawback is not too important.

The majority of florists keep bonsai indoors both for display and for storage. They may be kept in house plant conditions for some weeks prior to purchase and be in a weakened condition. In addition they may be over-watered to their detriment. Finally, the range is generally rather small and guidance on care offered is often rather meagre.

Buying at a horticultural show from a professional trader with a large exhibit of bonsai will offer the same advantages as purchasing from a specialist nursery. Such large exhibits can only be staged by a specialist and the trees offered for sale, though probably limited in quantity, are likely to represent the best currently available and to be in the correct price range. Competition for trade is keen at such shows and prices are likely to be very competitive. Advice on care is generally willingly given and fact-filled booklets of information will be available.

Bonsai clubs frequently hold raffles for members with trees as prizes, or have bring-and-buy sales with young trees on offer to help towards club funds. Bonsai or young trees obtained this way are generally healthy and well-rooted, though the quality of their training will depend on the skill and experience of the former owner. They are usually cheap and are generally in flower pots, yogurt cartons or similar containers.

Generally, in purchasing a bonsai from a professional source, the examples seen will represent good value for money. This is, of course, relative, and when looking at larger, older bonsai, which may cost £50 to £100 or more, it should not be forgotten that one is looking at the results of many years of highly skilled training and hundreds of hours of regular watering, feeding and potting. However, young trees that have good basic shape and the beginnings of a sturdy trunk can be frequently purchased, complete with their pot, for £4 to £10 as at the time of writing, and these offer an ideal way to obtain a number of different tree varieties, perhaps of Japanese species not easily obtainable in Britain.

BONSAI FROM SEED FOR INDOORS Flat dwellers who must, of necessity, cultivate warm-climate bonsai are rarely able to find young seedlings of suitable trees. However, seeds are easily purchased fresh in fruit from a greengrocer's shop (dried seeds of tropical varieties are often no longer viable), and a little forest of interesting and unusual kinds can be quickly grown.

GAINING EXPERIENCE As the months pass, a novice discovers that bonsai are not the mystical, difficult subjects they are often made out to be, but are, in fact, quite easy to grow. Sensing that there is more to learn, he may join a club. Due to their growing popularity and the frequency with which bonsai are exhibited (very few flower shows of any size in the United Kingdom are without a bonsai exhibit staged by one of the professional nurserymen) new clubs are being formed in many areas in Britain. At these, meetings are usually held on a monthly basis, local displays organised and outings to nurseries, arboreta or similar places of interest arranged. Members and guest lecturers help and advise newcomers and young trees are exchanged. For the beginner, joining a club is a good means of expanding his or her horizons. He will see trees bigger than he could imagine growing, watch a number of more experienced members potting or pruning, and gain valuable experience in a wider range of species than he would be likely, for a while, to own himself. However, bonsai training is also suited to those who prefer solitude and membership of a club is not essential. Learning is then by trial and error, observation, reading and, on occasions, asking questions. Many a pleasing collection has been developed by self-taught enthusiasts.

Following a degree of initial success, a collector may feel a need to see "real" bonsai. As has been said, there are very few full-time professional nurserymen who grow them in the United Kingdom, and for many people their first view will be of a mature imported Japanese bonsai in the flower marquee at their local agricultural show. Seeing a large, well-laid-out trade exhibit in such surroundings may create mixed feelings. Admiration certainly, but perhaps also resigned thoughts that the collector, with his two-year-old beech tree, will never achieve these standards. In such moments, the novice can be forgiven for not remembering that the owner or trainer of the specimens on show was an awestruck beginner once. Due to the comparatively short time that bonsai have been popular in Britain the tradition of family bonsai nurseries such as exist in Japan is not known. The leading collectors, both amateur and professional, could be described as self-taught, and once aware of this, exhibits of fine bonsai can be viewed by the novice in a different light. Instead of being overawed by the aged specimens he should try and develop his own ideas from these trees. It is an interesting exercise to endeavour to work out how an old bonsai has been trained, why it is the shape it is, and for what reason it is potted in a particular size and shape of pot. This is not easy at first but after a while the picture becomes more clear.

Three of the finest collections of bonsai in Britain are owned by women who have trained the trees themselves. In Japan, although women may water bonsai and perform other similar tasks, the famous collections are all owned by men, as are the professional nurseries. Traditions can be difficult to break and in the East, with its long history of a difference in status

Trees from the author's collection displayed at the Chelsea Flower Show, 1981.

between men and women, change may take some time, but the comparative newness of the hobby of bonsai in the United Kingdom and a different outlook on such things, has enabled both men and women to develop equal skills in this art form. In the three British collections just referred to there are many fine imported trees, considerably developed and improved by their owners, but including numerous English kinds, both small and large, which have been grown from seeds or cuttings or else collected as young or older trees from the wild. They also contain examples of plants obtained from specialist plant and shrub nurseries (a useful source of more unusual varieties) as additions to the range.

Specialists in any branch of horticulture are usually not only willing but pleased to talk to those with similar enthusiasm in their chosen field. There are, for instance, nurseries which specialise in the propagation and growing of ornamental shrubs and from which good healthy plants can be bought at a reasonable price and where information on habits, watering needs and so on can be obtained. The full potential of ornamental shrubs as bonsai has not yet been exploited in Britain and a wealth of attractive starting material is waiting for the inspired collector to experiment with.

Having grown bonsai for long enough to develop confidence in maintaining them in good health and reasonable shape, the ambitious collector is strongly advised to consider the purchase of a good Japanese-trained tree. Owning one or more of these is a certain way of raising the standard of all other trees in one's collection. However, the source of these is extremely limited, and perhaps only half a dozen bonsai nurserymen would be in a position to sell a reasonably mature, well-trained tree without unsightly faults, so the enthusiast should visit all these nurserymen before making a choice, as he is likely to be spending a considerable sum of money. Having given consideration to all the bonsai available, he should choose the one that at the same time impresses him, inspires him and appeals to him. He should not buy a tree he does not like, merely because he is told that it is a good bonsai, or because it is of a variety he does not have. Bonsai are, after all, an art form and exist to be looked at and enjoyed. With the purchasing of a good specimen, the collector is likely to turn to his own trees with renewed interest. As his knowledge increases he notices the potential beauty of more trees and plants. From time to time he may purchase another bonsai but his main energies are channelled into improving and developing those he has grown.

A collector experiences enormous satisfaction when he successfully transplants his first old, wild-grown tree and develops it into a beautiful bonsai. As has been said already, landowners are often willing to give permission for collectors to search for and dig up such trees on their property provided areas where gamebirds are reared are avoided and dogs are kept under control. Experience has shown that when a collector takes the trouble to write to thank landowners afterwards – whether or not he had been successful in his search – return visits are usually welcomed.

In all these ways a collection grows. Not only in numbers but in quality, diversity of shapes or styles and range of species. A collector may, for instance, try growing some of the tiny mame bonsai. In some ways the skills needed are applied differently from those for other forms of training. The growth of a mame bonsai must be very well controlled if the essential shaping of branches and trunk is to be maintained. Their watering needs can create difficulties until the collector learns to plunge the pots into trays of peat during the summer months. Of course, not every experiment has a successful conclusion. Some efforts will result in total failure, others will not turn out in the manner intended. One thing that is certain, however, is that every attempt to ''bonsai'' a tree will result in an increased knowledge, awareness, understanding and appreciation of how and why the process works.

CHAPTER THREE

PLANTS WHICH MAKE GOOD BONSAI

There are many species and varieties of hardy trees and shrubs readily available in the United Kingdom. Many of these are easily trained into good bonsai while others, generally considered less suited because of their leaf size, or growth habit, may occasionally be found growing in a most suitable way for training. Such opportunities should not be overlooked.

Many of the trees found in the British Isles are easily grown from seed. Others can be collected from the wild as small seedling trees or larger specimens growing in an attractive way, but it is very important to remember that permission must be obtained from the landowner, be it on moorland or anything else, before digging up young and especially older trees. Unlike some wild flowers it is not actually illegal to collect them provided the necessary permission has been obtained, but it could well be so if this is not done.

Small-leaved, naturally well-branched kinds, make an easy start to a collection. The elm, hornbeam, blackthorn, hawthorn and silver birch all fall into this category and seedlings are readily obtainable. Hawthorn grows a long taproot and resents initial disturbance, but once established in a pot is easy to care for and cultivate. Seedlings of small-leaved garden species, such as cotoneaster, pyracantha and laburnum are easily found and have the advantage that they will flower and, in the case of the first two, bear berries as well.

Trees with naturally larger leaves are usually trained into bonsai a foot or more high. This helps to compensate for the larger leaf size, although over a period of time this will be reduced considerably. Four of the nicest are easily grown from freshly-collected seed – oak, beech, horse chestnut and crab apple. Beech seed collected from copper beech trees will, with luck, produce copper-leaved seedlings in about five per cent of those germinating. These are especially attractive when trained if a seedling of a good dark colour is picked out. Oak seedlings vary enormously and it is worth selecting those which early on display the smallest and most deeply divided foliage. Horse chestnuts grow well, too well for some people, but with determination can be well-trained. They have the advantage of being almost indestructible. Crab apples make delightful bonsai. The seeds may be gathered from freshly-fallen crab apples, and if planted while fresh, germinate quickly and easily in a seed tray or flower pot. If a number are grown, a preliminary selection can be made in the first year, discarding those that show signs of mildew (some are susceptible) and retaining any with special features such

"THE SMALL ELM GROUP"

Zelkova serrata
Group Planting

This group of 13 *Zelkova serrata* (frequently referred to, incorrectly, as Japanese elm) was planted by the author in 1978. The two largest trees in the group were imported from Japan in 1973 and planted with a third to form a group in 1976 for exhibition at the Chelsea Flower Show of the following year. The idea of creating a group planting for this show each year was thus established and early in 1978 the 34 in (85 cm) long container was imported from Japan with this objective in mind. A number of English-grown zelkovas were selected to create the group, but the largest of these lacked the necessary substance and maturity. So the earlier group of three was split up and two of the Japanese trees used alongside eleven British ones to create a group representing a woodland scene.

Arranging and planting the group took some eight or nine hours. None of the trees were tied into position in any way, careful potting ensuring stability. Care was taken over the contours of the soil and the relationship of the trees, one to another, larger trees being positioned at the front of the group and somewhat elevated, the smaller trees being placed to the sides and rear. The container, at the time of planting probably the largest in Britain, is mid-brown Kataokaware, 34 in (85 cm) long and 17 in (42.5 cm) wide and 2½ in (6.5 cm) deep. The sides are outward-sloping and then strongly incurved, giving an elegant light appearance to a very large pot. The overall height of the group is 2 ft 4 in (70 cm), the largest tree being approximately 2 ft (60 cm) tall.

The planting has become known as "The Small Elm Group", despite its size. Due to the inspiration it gave to the author, and, incidentally, to many others, a still larger container 44 in (1.1 m) long and identical in shape, was imported during the winter of 1978/9 in order to create another such group. Meanwhile, the third bonsai of the original group was used in the planting of March, 1979, along with 18 English-grown Z. *serrata*, to form another group which was to become "The Large Elm Group". Displayed at Chelsea in 1979 but rarely shown outside London because of is weight, (around 200 lb (90 kg). This planting has a great effect on all who see it.

The ages of the trees in both groups range from about eight years to approximately 25 years. It is planned to re-pot them both early in 1982, as it was too wet and cold in 1981.

"THE SMALL ELM GROUP"

Zelkova serrata
Group Planting

"NICHOLAS"

Juniperus chinensis

"NICHOLAS"

Juniperus chinensis

This is an incredibly beautiful and very old bonsai ("Nicholas", because it was bought on Christmas Eve), obtained by the author in 1975 in a large, dark blue glazed rectangular pot which did not suit it. The foliage was sparse everywhere and the branch on the left swept the ground. The trunk was leaning backwards at an angle of 45 degrees and looked weary and green with age and neglect. So three days were spent wiring the neglected branches and removing completely those which spoilt the shape of the tree. During this process, it was propped up at the correct angle, and later it was re-potted. Exhibited at the Chelsea Flower Show in 1976, Japanese buyers made unsuccessful efforts to purchase it.

Attempts were made to obtain a more suitable pot for this magnificent tree. One pot in Japan of the correct size, shape and quality was not apparently available for purchase. However, it was perfectly suited to the tree and after lengthy correspondence and an exchange of photographs, it was eventually obtained and finally arrived in England in February, 1978. Despite some worry over re-potting again quite so soon, it was found that a good root-ball of vigorous roots had formed during the two-year interval and it was decided that the operation would anyway cause little disturbance. In March, 1978 the bonsai was potted into its new container, which is a silver fox-coloured, unglazed Yamaki pot, the curve of its sides reflected in the striking trunk of the tree, and the incurved lip giving it a well-finished appearance.

Further work was carried out to improve the shape of the areas of foliage which were now growing well. In addition, after years of neglect soil and debris had collected around the base of the trunk and numerous small roots had grown into this, covering the original wide-spreading roots and spoiling the base of the tree. The small roots have been removed one by one, so restoring the base to its former glory.

At present this bonsai, probably about 250 years old, stands about 3 ft 6 in (1.15 m) high (including the container) and is of a similar width. It has been exhibited at several shows in England and Wales, and on such occasions it is normally exhibited on a stand 36 in by 24 in by 12 in (1 m by 60 cm by 30 cm) made for it in London in 1976. This is worked in mahogany to a 17th century Japanese design.

Of all the bonsai owned by the author, this, if any one tree can be, is her favourite, its appearance being a constant inspiration and the quiet, dark green foliage having a peaceful, timeless air.

*A hawthorn (*Crataegus*) trained since 1975 in the windswept style from a wild
tree. It is now about 10 years old.*

as red leaves. Seedling crab apple trees will flower at three or four years of
age and respond well to training by wiring or pruning.

Among other flowering kinds are cherry, almond, peach and plum, all
members of the genus *Prunus* which can be grown from seed (the nut inside
the kernel). These are harder to shape and flower less readily than when full
sized and their long leaves are less desirable on bonsai. Almond is perhaps
the easiest of the four groups to grow to flowering size and has smaller
leaves than the other three. Seeds of all four may be slow to germinate and
a period of cold before planting will help to break dormancy.

For those wishing to try growing flowering bonsai from cuttings, forsythia,
winter jasmine and various of the quinces are worth while. They are easy to
root and have the advantage of flowering early in the year. The quince
flowers are effective for a longer period than most others and the colour
range of pink, orange or red is one not shared by many other suitable
ornamentals.

Lucky owners of a lime-free water supply – assuming that rainwater is not
readily available – can train azaleas as bonsai, the evergreen types responding
better to such training. Many of these are not completely hardy and should
be overwintered in cool greenhouse conditions. The varieties most favoured
for bonsai in Japan are those with smaller than average flowers, and it is,
alas, all too common in the West to see well-trained azalea bonsai with
flowers of too large a size. Azaleas are pruned very hard each year immedi-

Acer buergeranum *(left) and* A. palmatum *which have been grown from seed for bonsai training:*

ately after flowering and, by the time the following spring comes round, are again covered with a wealth of rich green leaves and beautiful flowers of many hues.

Willows of all sorts can be readily trained as bonsai. They are usually easy to root from cuttings and most are tolerant of standing for long periods in water, a bonus for the owner who must frequently be away from home. Alders can also stand in water. They tend to have rather large leaves, although these reduce over a time, but they respond well to training as medium to large bonsai.

Some trees are noted for their autumn colour, especially the Japanese and Canadian maples. Many of these can be obtained as young trees from garden centres and some can be grown from seed. The small-leaved Japanese *Acer palmatum* and *Acer buergeranum* are especially recommended. Other trees noted for their autumn colour and easily trained include the Japanese elm (*Zelkova serrata*) or, alternatively, the Judas tree (*Cercis siliquastrum*) and the similar, but much more unusual, katsura tree, *Cercidiphyllum japonicum*. All these can be grown from seed, as can the primitive ginkgo, a deciduous conifer, though this one is more often grown from cuttings or obtained as a young tree.

Among other conifers, two more deciduous kinds are readily available, the larches, including *Larix decidua* and *L. kaempferi*, which can be grown from seed, and the swamp cypress (*Taxodium distichum*), a water lover, easily

Larch (Larix decidua), *collected from the wild 17 years ago. The cones are up to four years old.*

grown from cuttings. The latter opens its "leaves" very late in spring to a bronze-red colour. Then, green all summer, the tree develops magnificent autumn colours before dropping the season's foliage and going into dormancy. The larch turns yellow in autumn and is of interest at that season, but it is perhaps seen at its best in late spring when its second soft, pale green young growth contrasts with the deeper green of the first growth of spring. It is also able to produce flowers and cones at four or five years of age, the latter staying on the tree for up to four years. The cones produce a quantity of fertile seed. This can be planted in the normal manner and the resulting seedlings can be used for bonsai training or for growing as full-size trees. In the space of a few years, the bonsai owner could easily create a family of larches, grown from seed produced by a slightly older bonsai.

The Scots pine, *Pinus sylvestris,* can be trained to become a good bonsai. Naturally straggly when young, it responds readily to wiring and bud removal. It is readily obtainable from seed. Young and old wild trees may also be found and can be transplanted provided great care is taken. Like those of many pines, the root system may not be very vigorous.

Among other evergreens, the holm oak, *Quercus ilex,* is one of the easiest to train. Readily grown from freshly collected acorns, it has very attractive, down-covered, silvery spring growth, contrasting well with the very dark green older foliage. It tolerates a wide range of soils and conditions and branches readily when trained.

The common box *Buxus sempervirens*, is easily trained and is especially suited to the smaller sizes of bonsai, as is the privet (*Ligustrum ovalifolium*) and its golden form (*aureum*). The common yew (*Taxus baccata*) and its golden form (*aurea*) can be trained into a small or large bonsai which will tolerate a rather shady position. It is extremely hard to grow from seed, but seedlings of *T. baccata* are freely available and it can be rooted from cuttings. It is as well to note that every part of a yew is poisonous.

Ivy (*Hedera helix*) is a less obvious candidate for bonsai training but both the species and the cultivated forms will, with a little effort, produce a woody trunk and an interesting shape. This need not be, as one might expect, in a cascading style. Ivies of many sorts can be trained to upright styles, regular pruning of long shoots preventing the usual weeping habit of ivy branches under the weight of their own foliage and the length of their growth. If they are kept compact, bark will begin to form on the trunk and then branches.

Young specimens of Taxodium distichum *(see page 68) which, when photographed, had only been grouped together for six weeks.*

Many ivies will tolerate shade but variegated forms should be kept in a light position to improve leaf colour. Ivy bonsai are not as hardy as one would expect and should be protected in winter in a cold greenhouse, porch or similar place.

The cedars (*Cedrus*) make fine bonsai when trained formally or informally to a height of about 24 in (60 cm). Their naturally spreading habit is an advantage when training and the results can be impressive. The Japanese cedar, *Cryptomeria japonica*, although very different in appearance from traditional cedars, is also eminently suited to formal training and has the bonus of turning a very striking bronze-red in the winter. It is vigorous, and with regular pinching out of growth during the spring and summer, good results can be obtained in a few years.

One evergreen that should be a "must" in every bonsai collection is the juniper. The common wild juniper, *Juniperus communis*, can be found in the more rugged and remote areas of Britain and fine specimens can be selected. They are very difficult to transplant when old, but younger plants are more amenable. They can be grown from cuttings. The Chinese juniper, *J. chinensis*, is even more suited to bonsai cultivation as it produces adult foliage as opposed to the rather spikey juvenile foliage of *J. communis*. Another, rarer juniper, is *J. rigida* (native to Japan, northern China and Korea), which naturally forms a small tree of weeping habit and can be trained into many bonsai styles. Its very hard, long, juvenile foliage has an attractive white line along the length of each needle, giving it a light overall appearace.

There have been many arguments on the merits or demerits of growing naturally dwarf trees, especially dwarf conifers, as bonsai. In general this practice is not desirable, although some forms growing only a few feet under natural conditions may successfully be trained as mame or miniature bonsai, under 6 in (15 cm) in height. All too frequently, completely untrained dwarf conifers are offered for sale as bonsai. To undertake real training of these naturally very slow growing trees is a task requiring many, many years of skill and perseverance.

There are, however, some relatively dwarf deciduous plants that can be trained to be good small or mame bonsai. Notable among these is *Betula nana*, the arctic birch, which has small leaves and can produce a nicely-shaped crown. Another less expected plant which makes a very beautiful mame bonsai is the spiraea. The common spiraea, *Spiraea japonica*, has heads of tiny pink flowers and green leaves, which are reddish-pink when young. Species such as *S. thunbergii* have on the other hand small, willow-like leaves and white flowers in early spring. *S. bumalda* 'Goldflame' has reddish-green and yellow variegated foliage and pink flowers in summer. So many spiraeas are worthy of cultivation as bonsai that a visit to a well-stocked garden centre to make a choice could be worth the time spent.

The well-known Virginia creeper, *Parthenocissus quinquefolia*, makes an unusual but beautiful bonsai, easy to train and worth keeping if only for its magnificent colour in autumn. If the very fine, almost tendril-like side shoots are regularly trimmed, it will rapidly form a woody trunk and branches and it is easily trained into upright, weeping or cascading styles, thus providing the enthusiast with many opportunities. While on the subject of climbing

LEFT: Chamaecyparis pisifera plumosa, *now 15 years old and 6in (15cm) high. This dwarf conifer would be approximately 18in (45cm) high and bushy in shape if it had been grown in a rock garden.*

RIGHT: *A specimen of* Spiraea japonica, *now 24 years old and 9in (23cm) high.*

plants, mention must be made of the lovely wisteria. Few who see this as a bonsai realise that it is trained with an upright or angled trunk, the weeping effect being created by the long, downward-sloping pinnate leaves and hanging racemes of flowers. There is only one satisfactory way to obtain a good wisteria for bonsai work and that is to air-layer (see Chapter 7) a sizeable and well-shaped section of a well-grown and floriferous plant. Growing from seed is never satisfactory as it may be many years before the seedling flowers, and plants purchased either from a garden centre, or from an importer of Japanese commercially-produced wisterias, are almost always grafted and a very unsatisfactory shape.

The reader will by now have realised that the range of trees suitable for bonsai training is very large indeed, but the scope can be further widened by looking for a moment at trees whose growth habit does not immediately lend itself to training but may, through circumstances, become very good bonsai indeed. The sycamore is one such. If grown from a seedling in normal conditions it is difficult to create from it that finely branched appearance so imperative to the good bonsai. It has, however, the ability to germinate and grow in the most unlikely places and, once growing, it rarely gives up, even when most other plants would die. When chance leads the collector to an interesting sycamore, well-dwarfed by freak growing conditions and with a good, thick, well-shaped trunk, it is an opportunity not to be missed. Provided special care is taken in transplanting, it will survive and thrive.

This **Acer pseudoplatanus** *is now many years old, but only under training as a bonsai for four years.*

Holly trees take a long time to train as bonsai of any size, and training can also be a somewhat painful process! Occasionally excellent material for holly bonsai can be obtained during the demolition of old holly hedges. Should such an opportunity occur, try to dig up a suitable plant in May or September, preferably the former, and be prepared to dig deep. Holly resents disturbance, but once a fine root system is developed, re-potting presents no problems. Given that the trunk is a nice shape, any unwanted growth can be removed, new shoots being readily produced. While soft and green these respond to wiring, and although hardy while growing in open ground, as a bonsai this is another plant which is best sheltered from the worst of the winter weather.

Plane trees and lime trees make interesting informal upright bonsai, as does the poplar. Plane trees' leaves respond well to bonsai training, reducing considerably in size after three or four years. The sweet chestnut is another large-leaved tree that does surprisingly well under cultivation in a pot, and all four of the trees mentioned may occasionally be discovered as good-sized specimens. All are widely used in towns and cities and many such places have large areas of common land within a short distance of streets where the trees are grown and in which they may seed themselves. One interesting feature of commons is that they are generally reclaimed bog or marsh and, as such, often have a water table only 3 or 4 in (8 or 10 cm) below the surface of the soil. Tree roots do not like the permanently saturated soil and spread outwards in the dryer top few inches. This makes digging them up (after permission has been obtained) an easy task and a tree from such a site may well have a nicely divided fibrous root system rather than the tap root associated with so many varieties. Unfortunately, it is often difficult to establish ownership of common land, but if you cannot establish it the answer is simple. Leave the seedlings where they are.

For those with a very limited space to devote to bonsai, and an inclination towards mame bonsai, there are, as well as the plants already mentioned, a number of suitable subjects, both hardy and half-hardy, to be found in a good alpine nursery. Some of these such as *Crassula sarcocaulis* are described in Chapter 10, but there are many others which offer a wide range of leaf size and colour, flowers and berries. For instance heathers and heaths embrace a wide range of foliage colour, habit and flower. With the exception of *Erica carnea* and a few others including *E. darleyensis* and *E. mediterranea*, all the ericas and the closely-related callunas favour lime-free conditions. Do not overlook the daphnes either, many of which are worth growing for their beautifully scented flowers. These are suitable for growing on alkaline soils.

Then there are a number of fairly hardy fuchsias which are a pleasure to train. An easy one to begin with is the *Fuchsia magellanica pumila*, which has small foliage and neat red flowers. It is best over-wintered in a cold greenhouse. There is also a large number of hebes, some of which make good small bonsai. They tolerate a wide range of soil conditions but while some are fully hardy, many are dubiously so and will need winter protection in most parts of the country.

Hypericums offer a wide choice, from the tiny *Hypericum reptans*, which carries solitary yellow flowers during the summer, to the variegated-leaved *H.* x *moseranum* 'Tricolor' with white, pink and green variegated leaves which also bears yellow flowers in summer. These shrubs like a well-drained soil and a sunny position.

Euonymus can also be trained as bonsai. Some of the newer variegated forms have better natural growth habits than the bigger older forms, and the cultivar *Euonymus fortunei* 'Emerald and Gold' has bright gold variegated leaves, tinged with an attractive pink shade in winter. In Japan *Euonymus fortunei* is often trained for the beauty of its autumn foliage, its fragrant blossoms and its berries. The tree is unfortunately not hardy, and it is essential to give it some protection during the colder months of the year. The winged spindle, *Euonymus alatus*, and the spindle tree itself, *E. europaeus*, are also trained as bonsai – both are deciduous – and are perhaps seen at their best in autumn, when the colour of their foliage can be said to vie with the maple in brilliance and intensity. Again, it must be noted that spindle trees are also very sensitive to cold in the later months of the year. If affected by this, the shoots will die back and this will be the more marked if the tree has not been adequately fed during the summer months.

The rock rose or *Cistus* can be trained to make flowering bonsai but care should be taken during selection to see them in flower and to choose small-flowered varieties. Nor can one ignore the cotoneasters, for there are many besides the deciduous *Cotoneaster horizontalis*. This species actually has an attractive, less rampant variegated form, but also worthy of consideration are *C. microphyllus* with large, bright red fruits and its variety *thymifolius*; also, of larger size, *C. simonsii* which develops an attractive silver trunk. The first two are evergreen, the last semi-evergreen. Enthusiasts should also check among the berberis and potentillas for yet more material, as the range is great.

One hazard that is frequently overlooked by the bonsai owner is that of dirty, polluted air. Many species do not respond favourably to this modern hazard but one tree that is more tolerant than most of these conditions is the Sakhalin spruce, *Picea glehnii*. This is both dense and bushy, and is frequently used for bonsai to good effect. The Sawara cypress, *Chaemaecyparis pisifera*, is unlike the many dwarf forms which are derived from it and forms a vast tree in Japan. It will grow rapidly and it is frequently found in both upright and twin-truck bonsai plantings in its native land.

Suggestions for suitable bonsai material would be incomplete without mention of other conifers which grow very large in their native lands and yet, as bonsai, are suited to cultivation in a wide range of sizes. The first is the redwood, native to the forest belts of the western United States. The Californian redwood, *Sequoia sempervirens*, is the world's tallest tree. The bark is mahogany-coloured and the dark green evergreen foliage is easily pinched out to promote the branched growth needed for a bonsai. *Sequoiadendron giganteum*, is the Wellingtonia or big tree, as it is also called. The largest known specimen is the world's largest (though not quite the tallest) living thing. This species has a furrowed reddish-brown trunk and responds well to the pinching out of foliage. Both this and the Californian redwood make excellent formal upright style bonsai and, grown in containers, should be given cold greenhouse protection in winter.

The third member of the redwood family is the fossil-age dawn redwood, *Metasequoia glyptostroboides* – native to central China – which was re-discovered in a remote part of that country in 1941. It also responds well to training, and the feathery foliage, similar to that of the swamp cypress, turns an attractive warm gold in autumn.

The nothofaguses or southern beeches (related to the beech and mostly from South America although some are native to Australasia) can also be trained as small or large bonsai. The most readily obtainable species is *Nothofagus procera* and results under bonsai training are fast, for a young tree in open ground is capable of reaching a height of 40 ft (12 m) in seven years. It is fairly easily grown from seed.

And so it goes on. The list can never be complete, but hopefully the aspiring bonsai trainer has by now realised that he need not search far for suitable material with which to pursue his hobby.

CHAPTER FOUR

A MONTHLY

CULTURAL GUIDE

To ensure that a bonsai lives a long and healthy life it is necessary to tend it in a number of ways, the type of attention differing with the time of year.

Both the novice and the more experienced collector alike should always try to remember that the advice and guidance available to them is only of use if it is adapted as need be to the varying needs of a particular bonsai. A tree is a living thing and there may be times in which it can be said to be not growing well for some reason and looking dull. It is, therefore, essential that the owner learns to know his trees intimately so that any changes which occur will be quickly noticed and corrected before too much damage has been caused. This type of response will come in time as a result of regular observation of bonsai and other trees and shrubs. Also developing from this will be an understanding of the way in which the plants grow and thrive.

If it should happen that a bonsai appears to be ailing, the owner should examine the tree very closely in case there is some insect infestation or disease. Should the bonsai prove to be free of either of these problems, the owner should try to remember recent weather conditions and whether there have been sudden extremes of temperature, excessive constant rain, or perhaps a period of drought, which may often go unnoticed in colder weather. Often through this process of elimination the cause of the problem may be discovered and prompt and appropriate action can be taken.

To help the novice collector care for his trees, the procedures for potting, watering, feeding and other matters are set out below on a monthly basis. But weather conditions vary in different parts of the country and it should be understood that the guidance given is appropriate for the London area in an average year. Those living in more northerly districts should bear in mind that procedures carried out in spring are tied in with the start of tree growth in response to warmth and increasing day length, and should delay them accordingly. Autumn care may also need to be brought forward in the same way. (*See end-papers for information on world-wide monthly temperature and rainfall figures.*)

JANUARY

This is usually the coldest month of the year and dubiously hardy trees should be in winter quarters. Depending on the tree, this might be underneath shelving or staging in a greenhouse, or in a cold frame. Coniferous and other evergreen trees should be overwintered under some simple form

*Simple structures for over-
wintering coniferous and hardy
deciduous bonsai. The trees are
protected from snow by a simple
roof and are standing on a
wooden plank raised off the
ground.*

of protection as snow could cause damage to branches by its weight. Snowy periods are otherwise not a problem, for once pots and trees are covered they rarely dry out and are insulated against sudden severe frost. Occasionally, due to a belt of cold air from the Arctic or Siberia, one experiences several consecutive days of extremely cold and often windy weather. Day and night temperatures do no rise even to freezing point and conditions are usually dry. This weather is not good for any potted tree and all bonsai should be sheltered temporarily. During these and all other dry, windy periods in winter they should be checked on alternate days to see if they need watering. Should this be the case, water should be given at around mid-day if possible, or else during the morning, but not in the evening.

Warm-climate bonsai which will be kept indoors will be relatively inactive at this time of year due to the lack of light, for they need both light and warmth for the encouragement of active growth. When the central heating system is on, insect pests may, however, be in evidence and such bonsai should be regularly inspected so that any infestation may be discovered and quickly dealt with. Indoor evergreen bonsai frequently become dusty at this time of year and therefore they look less attractive. This may be rectified by gently cleaning the foliage with water sprayed from a shower attachment or similar device. The temperature of the water should be set at tepid in order to prevent shock to the bonsai.

FEBRUARY

Conditions being generally similar to those in January, there are few new tasks to undertake. The flowering Japanese apricot (*Prunus mume*) may flower or may have already flowered, and will be developing leaves, so cold greenhouse or cold-frame treatment should, therefore, be continued. In a warm year, the flowering crab apples may also begin breaking into leaf. They, unlike the apricot, need little protection other than shelter from wind. If the month is excessively wet and the temperatures low, it is worth protecting trees from rain for a time to enable them to dry partially. Long, wet, cold winters are probably responsible for far more bonsai losses than are short periods of considerable cold.

In anticipation of spring potting and re-potting, soil supplies should be checked and, if necessary, orders for them placed. They should be prepared for the potting season by storing in a dry place, opening sacks to dry the contents. Re-potting is far easier with bone-dry soil.

Trees requiring re-potting should be inspected regularly to watch for signs of swelling of the buds. This indicates that the tree is starting to grow and it is at this stage, in the coming month, that re-potting should take place.

MARCH

The days are beginning to lengthen and temperatures to rise, although winter is far from past and wind can reach high speeds. Most trees will be coming out of their dormancy and buds will be swelling on many varieties. Some, however, will still be dormant, including both beech and ginkgo. As re-potting is the major task in March the methods by which it should be done and the reasons for doing it will be explained here.

Any tree growing in a container will, after a shorter or longer period, become pot-bound. This is, of course, because the roots grow, as well as the branches. Even when a tree is branch and twig pruned as drastically as many bonsai are, this does not stop the roots growing. However, unlike most pot plants, a bonsai is not necessarily potted on into a larger container. It is, rather, root-pruned and potted back into the same pot.

The part of a root of most use to a tree is the tip, which has the ability to absorb dissolved mineral salts from the soil. These pass along the length of the root to the tree, where they are used in growth. Root pruning has two effects. First, the distance between the root tip and the base of tree is shortened, which does not affect the tree in any way and secondly a pruned root, like a pruned branch, forms several side shoots which, each having a growing tip capable of absorbing substances from the soil, thus make the root more efficient. So a bonsai which is root-pruned will be found to have a root-ball consisting of short, actively growing, fine roots.

A bonsai ready for root-pruning should be somewhat dry and definitely not soaking wet. When lifted out of its pot some roots may be winding around the outside of the root-ball. These may be unwound and removed. The tree should then be placed on a board on a table and the outer areas of root-ball teased out and freed from soil. In the case of deciduous trees, up to one-third of the root-ball can be treated in this way, but with coniferous trees one quarter is preferable. The freed roots will hang down like an untidy fringe. These should be cut off with a clean, sharp pair of scissors, leaving a root-ball of reduced size which has cut root ends protruding a little. Wrap

(Continued on p. 54)

Re-potting step-by-step

PREPARING THE ROOT-BALL

RIGHT: *A pot-bound tree* (Pinus thunbergii). *Netting covering the holes in the base of the pot is deeply embedded in the root-ball.*

BELOW: *The outer, long roots of the bonsai specimen being freed and the soil gently loosened.*

BOTTOM: *Teasing out the root-ball.*

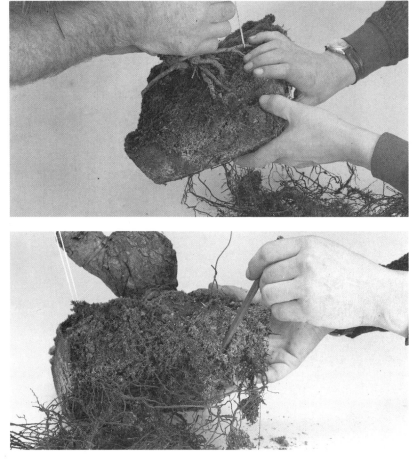

LEFT: *Over-long roots being removed.*

ABOVE: *Trimming back other roots to make the root-ball neater.*

LEFT: *The root-ball ready for re-potting.*

(See also p. 55)

"SALVADOR DALI"

Acer palmatum
Japanese mountain maple

Imported from Japan as one of a batch of small, 15-year-old maples in 1959, this tree was obtained by a collector who did much to improve its crown. In 1970 it was given to another collector who continued its training, but who passed it on to the author in 1973.

At the time, the tree had a slightly larger crown than at present, but lacked dignity at the base, due to the unfortunate placing of a small, round stone between the divided trunk. It was, however, due to this that the bonsai received its name of Salvador Dali, the divided trunk being reminiscent of paintings of human thighs by that famous artist.

To improve this part of the tree, a piece of limestone was obtained from the Cheddar Gorge area and broken into two pieces. These were shaped to fit either side of the base, giving the effect of a single piece of rock, over which the tree had grown for many years. In 1977 the crown was reduced by about 1 in (2.5 cm) as it had looked somewhat top-heavy.

Going back to 1973, the bosai was then potted into an apple green, glazed, rectangular container, giving it a reasonable appearance though the pot was 1 in (2.5 cm) deeper than the present very elegant Yamaki container, which measures 13 in (32.5 cm) by 9 in (23 cm) by 2½ in (6.5 cm). The current overall height is 16 in (40 cm).

"Salvador Dali" features in all the author's Chelsea Flower Show exhibits. To prepare it, as the show is held during the third week in May each year, the tree is encouraged to come into leaf in March, a month early, and fed lightly but regularly for three weeks. It is totally leaf pruned at the end of April and then placed on heated staging to encourage the growth of a new set of leaves. Watering is rigidly controlled during this period. The resulting leaves are small and of a red-brown colour, these becoming dark green later in the year before finally turning for a few brief days in autumn to a range of fiery reds and yellows.

"SALVADOR DALI"

Acer palmatum
(Japanese mountain maple)

"THE POMEGRANATE"

Punica granatum
(pomegranate)

"THE POMEGRANATE"

Punica granatum
(pomegranate)

This very fine and unusual bonsai has size, stature and a most remarkable trunk. Its small, attractive foliage is seen at its best in spring, when the emerging shoots and leaves are bronze-red, or in autumn, when the foliage turns a clear yellow before falling.

It was imported from Japan during the 1960s by the late General Sir Oliver Leese, the finest bonsai in his collection and exhibited by him at Chelsea Flower Show shortly before his death. It then passed into the hands of an amateur collector who developed the tree considerably. He made the interesting discovery that the centre of the trunk was filled with a cement-like material and removed this, little by little. The bonsai subsequently changed hands again and was allowed to grow considerable amounts of foliage. This improved the crown but rather detracted from the branches. At that time, the pomegranate was in an elegant, deep, square container, the sides flowing upwards and outwards, but as a result of the large amounts of twig growth allowed to develop, it became too small for the tree.

When it came into the author's collection the surface soil was covered with liverwort (indicative of bad drainage), and the tree was infested with scale insect. This was because it was growing then in a large fibre-glass pot (non-porous and therefore not really suitable for bonsai). At that time it was nearly dormant, so it was decided to clean the scale insect first. The liverwort was cleared from the top of the soil and, by careful attention to watering, waterlogging was prevented, so putting off temporarily the necessity of re-potting such a weak bonsai.

Once healthy, the tree was re-potted into a shallower, rectangular Yamaki pot 18 in x 14 in x 5 in (45 x 35 x 13 cm) still with the sloping, flared sides of the former, elegant container. Some very substantial pruning was carried out in order to improve the shape of the branches, and this, combined with the re-potting, invigorated it and it is now growing well. It is over-wintered on a heated greenhouse bench in a cool greenhouse and is moved out of doors once frost danger is over.

It has been exhibited at several shows, including the Chelsea Flower Show in 1981, and, at the time of writing, measures 34 in (85 cm) in height. It is always referred to as "The Pomegranate", being the only one of any size in the owner's collection.

this in a damp cloth to prevent drying out while the pot is prepared.

The pot, once washed, is ready for use. The drainage holes, which are large, can be covered with plastic mesh netting to prevent soil falling out, or worms entering. The traditional crocks (broken pieces of flower-pot) can be used, but in a small container they take valuable soil space and, being curved, may not be too efficient. In pots, other than the tiniest, or with trays less than 1 in (2.5 cm) deep, a layer of clean gravel chips will serve to cover the bottom of the pot to facilitate perfect drainage. Some dry potting mixture should then be added and at this stage the tree can be placed in the container to check that it is at the correct level. Any small height adjustments should be made at this stage, and then more potting soil added around the root-ball. The aim is to ease compost in among the roots rather than piling it on top and pressing down hard vertically and then easing more soil into the spaces created.

When enough compost has been added to give the necessary gentle slope upwards from the pot rim to the base of the trunk, a very fine layer of sieved top-soil can be added, sprinkling it on and spreading it with a soft brush. This facilitates the growing of moss on the soil surface. The tree should now be watered, using a mist spray or a watering can with a fine rose, until water runs out of the drainage holes at the bottom. The pot should be stood out of doors in a shaded spot, well sheltered from the wind and watered only when becoming dry until the tree is re-established. No fertiliser should be given for four to six weeks after re-potting.

Choosing the correct potting compost is of considerable importance. Bonsai trees require a compost that is free-draining and free from large lumps or dusty particles. Large lumps take up valuable space; dusty particles compact down and interfere with drainage. There are almost as many recommended types of compost as there are bonsai, yet the novice and the more experienced collector alike in the United Kingdom prefer to use a fairly standard combination of three or four ingredients for most of their potting needs. Suitable base ingredients are lime-free loam,* leaf-mould (well rotted oak or beech leaf-mould is best for deciduous trees, pine needle leaf-mould for coniferous trees), moss peat and clean sharp sand or fine grit. Loam varies a great deal and one not too rich in organic matter is preferable.

The loam and leaf-mould can be collected from out of doors if there is a suitable nearby source, but they should then be sterilised. A simple way of doing this for small quantities is to put them in a biscuit tin with a lid on and to roast them well in the oven. All ingredients should be sieved to remove large lumps, and they are then ready to mix as required.

The vast majority of broad-leaved deciduous trees thrive on this combination of loam, leaf-mould and grit, mixed in equal parts by volume, which is referred to as a standard compost mixture (for bonsai) in the Glossary of Plants (pp. 152 to 181). Conifers and other evergreens prefer an even better-drained mixture consisting of two parts by volume leaf-mould and grit

---

* Most trees suitable for training as bonsai tolerate lime but it is advisable to use lime-free loam, especially in areas where the water is hard. Experience has proved to the author that attention to this detail makes a significant difference to the health of the plants.

LEFT: *The tree is placed in the pot and its height and position checked.*

BELOW: *The tree potted and ready for watering.*

to one of loam and this is referred to in the Glossary as the coniferous compost mixture. Peat can be added for lime-hating plants such as azaleas, one part of peat being added to two of leaf-mould, two of grit and one of loam.

For the propagation of cuttings (both softwood and hardwood), a mixture of one part of peat to one of grit helps to ensure good rooting and provides well drained conditions for both coniferous and deciduous shoots.

During this month a check should be made to be sure that insecticides are at hand for use when required. Seeds should be sown in trays, labelled, and placed where mice and cats cannot reach them. Wild trees may also be dug up (with permission, see p. 22) and potted at this time of year.

APRIL

A variable month with warm pleasant days alternating with periods of cold, heavy rain and some frosts. Snow is not unknown.

Hardy trees should no longer require protection from the elements, although if a period of warm weather brings trees into leaf, be prepared to take frost precautions. A simple frost-protector for a tree in leaf is a sheet or two of old newspaper placed over it and held in place by the weight of a length of net curtain draped over the top. Frosty nights are rarely windy enough to dislodge this light but effective covering, which prevents ugly blackening of the leaves and the die-back of soft young shoots, both of which are detrimental to the bonsai. During warm spells, trees will need watering, possibly daily. At this time of year their water requirement increases considerably as they start growing.

Bonsai, other than those recently re-potted, should be fed in April. There is a vast range of fertilisers available but, with the exception of flowering and fruiting trees, whose feeding should relate to the time of production of a "crop", bonsai do well on a well-diluted general purpose fertiliser applied from April until July. From July onwards it is preferable to change to a fertiliser geared to fruiting plants, such as tomato feed, so that twigs ripen ready for winter. Otherwise, late growing sappy growth can be damaged by autumn frosts.

Flowering bonsai expected to set fruit benefit from the sparing use of tomato feed before they bloom. Then they should not be given any fertiliser until six weeks after flowering as earlier application would cause the fruits to drop off. After that period they can be fed for a few weeks with a general purpose fertiliser, before switching back to a tomato feed to ripen the wood.

In the main, April is too early for trees to be growing elongated shoots. In a mild year, however, growth may be starting and shoot-nipping must be carried out.

MAY

All bonsai should be in active growth as the weather continues to improve, though night frosts can still catch out the unwary and torrential rain is not unknown. In general, however, warmer dry days will predominate and a daily check should be made to see if watering is necessary whenever there is no rain. This may be an imprecise statement, but it is not possible to stipulate, for instance, the number of times per week to water. So much depends on whether the conditions obtaining are windy or sheltered, dry or humid, very sunny or only moderately so. Also, individual trees and species have different needs. One may be more vigorous than another, and the size of the pot and composition of the potting mixture are other factors to be taken into consideration. The ideal way to water bonsai, is to give water until it runs out of the drainage holes and then leave alone until the soil is becoming dry but is not completely so. At that stage water freely again. During the warmer months this could be interpreted as watering thoroughly in the morning and then checking in the evening to see if any of the pots have become dangerously dry during the day. If they have, water again.

With all bonsai growing new young shoots, May brings a number of undesirable insect visitors. Chief among these are greenfly or aphis which, given a spell of mild weather, multiply alarmingly. This rapid increase in numbers is due to the fact that not only are young produced by the normal egg-laying method requiring both male and female, but during the warmer months the female produces additional young, wingless greenfly by a process of parthenogenesis, a method of asexual reproduction. Greenfly are attracted by the sugary sap in the young tender shoots and feed by sucking this out through the soft stem tissues. A severe infestation can, therefore, seriously weaken a growing tree. Plants most likely to be attacked are maples, and unfortunately many maple bonsai are intolerant of chemical sprays, however mild. So provided bonsai are not large, a suitable and safe method of greenfly removal is to fill a bucket with water to which has been added a desertspoonful of washing-up liquid, in which the tree may be held upside down, its crown and branches submerged and gently moved around. This should remove all the greenfly; any left can be removed by hand.

Indoor bonsai will by now be in full growth and it is essential to attend regularly to their trimming and watering. By the end of the month (or early in June in the coldest areas) even the tropical varieties can usually be safely stood outside for three months if space is available, as they will benefit from a spell in the fresh air and the sunshine. Where this is not possible, the trees can be placed by open windows. Bonsai which have been kept indoors and which are given this change of environment may, after a short period of adjustment, enter a stage in which growth activity is considerable and their water requirements will increase dramatically. A careful watch should, therefore, be maintained to ensure that their needs are supplied.

Pests are at their most active; prompt action should be taken.

JUNE

Traditionally a hot and sunny month when all bonsai are growing, and both pruning and watering must be attended to regularly. Conifers such as jun-

LEFT: *A* Cryptomeria japonica *raft planting allowed to grow and change its style.* RIGHT: *After initial pruning the potential shape can be seen.*

ipers and cryptomeria will require daily pinching out of developing shoots to maintain a compact bushy appearance, and deciduous trees such as maple and zelkova require the removal or shortening of their shoots. Soft shoots of secondary growth may be used as cuttings, to be rooted under mist or in similar conditions. These should be taken with a heel of older wood attached.

At this time of year, many collectors move their trees into a shadier position in the mistaken belief that they require protection from the sun. However, bonsai are not a special species or variety but simply ordinary trees whose small stature has been induced by training. The vast majority require sunshine to produce healthy, short-jointed growth and foliage does not burn in bright sunshine if adequate humidity can be provided as well. The only reason why bonsai may sometimes be shaded in summer is to cut down on excessive watering. Wiring of branches can be carried out on deciduous trees and on coniferous bonsai other than pines in June and July. Wire should be carefully applied to avoid trapping leaves, which could rot and attract disease.

Deciduous trees can be intentionally defoliated completely during June (see Chapter 7), to cause the growth of a second set of smaller, richer-coloured leaves. Bonsai undergoing this treatment must be carefully watered.

Weeds are an annual summer problem. Young seedlings among the bonsai trees should be removed at once to prevent root disturbance. Greenfly should still be watched for throughout June, and during wet spells slugs and snails may be about in some numbers. Slug bait seems to attract slugs from nearby gardens so a better remedy is to present your slug pellets to garden-proud neighbours and to trap your own slugs in jam jars containing a little stale beer. In dry spells red spider can attack junipers and other trees and an appropriate systemic insecticide should be used immediately their presence is noted – though not, as we already noted, on maples. They are less likely to appear where bonsai are kept reasonably humid.

JULY

Conditions for established bonsai are similar to those prevailing in June, and care and cultivation must continue in a similar manner. Rooted softwood cuttings taken earlier may be potted on into small training pots and be placed outside in a sheltered, humid place. July is traditionally holiday time, many people going away for two or three weeks. Neighbours are often a great help when this happens, perhaps watering your vegetable garden and herbaceous border, but unless they are accustomed to the needs of bonsai in very hot weather they may accidentally allow the trees to die. However, more than one collector has entrusted bonsai to his neighbours, encouraging them to learn about them, and subsequently mutual holiday bonsai-watering arrangements have worked well for both parties.

An alternative solution for those with garden space to spare is to dig holes in the ground in a damp and shady area. In these, the bonsai can be buried up to their first branch while still in their pots. The area containing the bonsai can be thoroughly soaked by leaving a hose running slowly into it for several hours and under the conditions this creates the trees will survive periods of up to a month of hot weather without permanent damage. Deciduous trees should be thoroughly pruned before leaving them, but upon your return they will need pruning again to remove etiolated growth and there may well be worms in the pots. These can be removed by standing the pots in a bowl of water so that the water level is above the soil level. The worms, to avoid drowning, come out of the root-ball. At the same time the bonsai is quickly restored to its former beauty.

For those whose collection has grown so large that there is no spare room for it in the garden, an automatic watering system is useful. In this, a number of mist jets are connected to a tap and controlled by a timing clock. The mist can be pre-set to come on for an hour both morning and evening, and this amount of watering should cope with even very hot spells. The disadvantage is that, without great sophistication and the setting up of an elaborate,

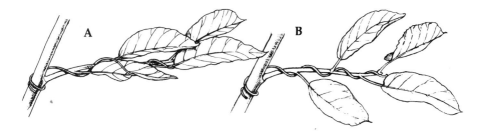

A. *An incorrectly wired branch. The leaves must not be trapped by the wire.* **B.** *The correct wiring for a branch in leaf.*

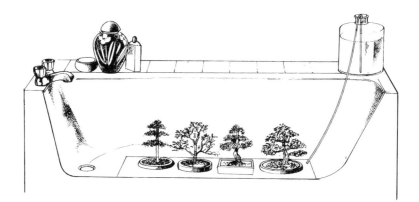

Indoor bonsai (and house plants) standing on capillary matting in a bath. Fine tubing leading from the water container provides a slow trickle of water to the matting.

expensive system, it is difficult to arrange for it to switch itself off when it is raining and, on occasions, the bonsai may be over-watered. In summer this is less of a problem than in winter, and for the period involved should not harm the trees unduly.

Flat dwellers with indoor or outdoor bonsai can with advantage buy a piece of capillary matting. This is a man-made substance, in appearance like a thin blanket, that absorbs a large amount of water. It can be placed on the bottom of a bath and thoroughly soaked, and the bonsai are then stood on it, and pressed into it as much as possible.

There are two ways in which the matting can be kept moist. First, a large bowl of water is placed in the shallow end of the bath and the end of the capillary matting is placed in this so that it touches the bottom of the bowl. Water seeps along the matting and any surplus runs down the plug-hole.

Alternatively, take a large water carrier such as is used by campers and place this on the edge of the shallow end of the bath. The water carrier will have to have a piece of rubber tubing of small bore fitted to drip water from the carrier to the capillary matting. This rubber tube is then led to the capillary matting. The rate of water flow will be governed by the internal diameter of the tube. A teaspoon per gallon (4.5l) of Jeyes Fluid should be added to the water to prevent algae forming and blocking the fine tubing.

The bathroom curtains should be left closed so that the room remains cool, and in these conditions the trees will survive well. However, experiments should be carried out prior to holiday time to ensure that the trickle from the bottle remains constant and that it is large enough to maintain a water supply over the necessary period.

AUGUST

Bonsai will not grow so fast in August and will require less pruning, although temperatures may still be high. Watering must still be attended to although the need may be less, due to dew forming at night.

Semi-hardwood cuttings may be taken for rooting under glass, but it is too late for softwood cuttings to become rooted and established before the onset of winter induces dormancy. Feeding should be carried out with well-diluted fertilisers of the tomato-feed type to encourage ripe wood that will tolerate autumn frosts. Frequency of feeding should be reduced and stopped completely next month.

Coniferous trees can be re-potted this month if necessary and willows, whose fast-growing root systems may necessitate twice-yearly re-potting, should also be root-pruned and re-potted if examination indicates the need.

Wild trees may be lifted (see p. 31 regarding the necessity for obtaining permission to do this) and potted up towards the end of the month. They will still have time to establish themselves before the onset of winter.

Some of the most tender of the tropical bonsai that have been outdoors during the summer months will now need to be brought in before the dark evenings lengthen any further and the nights become cold. So watch should be kept on such trees, which is made easier if the owner has a horticultural maximum-minimum thermometer located near his bonsai. By regular reading of this, falling night temperatures will be noted and the appropiate action can be taken.

SEPTEMBER

The bonsai will no longer be growing so the need for pruning is minimal. Wiring should not be carried out, but ready-wired branches can be checked to see if they are set and, if they are, the wires can be removed. In the southern counties of Britain bonsai will not as yet be showing their autumn colours but internal chemical changes will be taking place to prepare the tree for dormancy.

The weather is frequently fine and dry, although cold at night and night frosts are a possibility. Watering is still necessary but dew and morning mists reduce this to a less regular task. Wild trees and conifers can still be transplanted and potted and hardwood cuttings can be prepared for planting.

Preparations for the over-wintering of less hardy trees should be initiated and tender species which have spent the summer out of doors should be moved into a cool greenhouse.

Woodland trees are beginning to shed their seeds and good trees of desired varieties should be closely watched for these. Seeds can be sown in seed trays and left out of doors to stratify throughout the winter, though the trays should be netted against the attentions of cats and mice.

OCTOBER

With luck, the weather may well remain fine during this month. Deciduous trees will be showing the brilliance of their autumn colours. As leaves fall they should be removed from pots and shelves, for if neglected they become a refuge for slugs, woodlice and many other undesirable creatures. All tender trees should be under cover by now.

Bonsai should still be watered regularly in dry periods, but their demands are lessening and the dews and morning mists may provide most of the daily needs.

More wild seeds can be collected and planted. Some can be stored for stratification and planting in early spring.

Pine bonsai occasionally become infested with woolly aphis. You will see what looks like tiny pieces of cotton wool at the base of the needles. A minor infestation can be dealt with by dabbing the affected parts with cotton wool buds dipped in methylated spirits, but a more extensive infestation can be removed by spraying.

NOVEMBER

There is very little activity in November and watering should be minimal. The last leaves of deciduous trees will fall and should be cleared away and the trees moved to their over-wintering quarters.

DECEMBER

The quietest month of the year. Bonsai should be checked two or three times a week in case there are drying winds, but generally little needs to be done. It is an ideal time to increase one's knowledge by reading, not only bonsai books but books on trees around the world. Study photographs of bonsai, especially where a series of shots, taken over a few years, demonstrates the changes that have taken place in the appearance of the trees.

On dry and mild days, deciduous bonsai can with advantage be taken from the position in which they are over-wintering and be placed on a turntable at a convenient viewing height. This enables them to be carefully studied. It is important to do this at this time of year as it is impossible during the summer months when foliage abounds. But the delicate tracery of the branches is now clearly visible from all angles and its faults and virtues are readily seen, so decisions on pruning can be made and acted on later at the appropriate time.

MAME BONSAI

Mame bonsai require slightly different cultivation and care from larger bonsai. Their training is dealt with in Chapter 6 (p. 110).

As they are growing in very tiny pots, there is always a danger of their becoming too dry. The soil mixture should, therefore, be altered to one with less leaf-mould and sand, though ericaceous plants must have plenty of leaf-mould in their potting mixture and should, accordingly, be watched especially carefully.

The soil mixture should be finely sieved and be dry at the time of re-potting. All roots touching the sides of the pot should be cut off and up to two-thirds of the soil in the root-ball removed. A small, slim chopstick is a useful aid when teasing out mame bonsai root-balls. More soil and root may be safely removed from deciduous than from coniferous bonsai specimens.

The repotting procedure is as for larger trees, but once re-potted, mame bonsai may be placed with advantage in a cold-frame or cold greenhouse for a few weeks to recover from the shock of transplanting and become re-established in their pots.

Watering, especially during the summer months, is an important aspect of mame bonsai care. It is customary for British enthusiasts to stand the little pots on damp sand, or partially bury the pots in damp peat so that the trees do not die as a result of drying out during a hot day while the owner is at work. This is a practical and sensible solution to a problem, but it should be said that it is detrimental to the growth of the mame bonsai. There is a tendency with such overwatering for roots to grow through the drainage hole into the cool moist sand or peat. They rapidly become thick and coarse and top growth is correspondingly large and disproportionate. The constant supply of moisture encourages too much growth in a tree that is meant to remain small.

Mame bonsai maintained in the most ideal way should be given as little water as possible while still maintaining life and health. In this way, any growth will be short-jointed and in correct proportion to the tree. Fertilisers are used sparingly but regularly, a healthy bonsai being the objective. Liquid fertilisers are easiest to apply and those used for fruiting plants, such as tomatoes, are preferable as they do not encourage the growth of green sappy shoots, but rather the production of ripe wood.

During the winter months, mame bonsai should be given the protection of a cold frame. Otherwise the roots, being in such small pots, are vulnerable to constant freezing and thawing which will cause breaking of the root cells. But during the summer they should, like other trees, receive plenty of sunshine, and if a humid microclimate can be maintained around them the problems of watering are lessened.

The reader may feel, after reading this month by month account of bonsai care, that the work and time involved is considerable. Far from this being the case, the tasks can be fitted in easily with other activities and the trees themselves impart a feeling of calm and tranquillity which is an added bonus.

CHAPTER FIVE

BONSAI FOR INDOORS

The novice bonsai owner frequently keeps his first tree indoors. In Britain, at least, this may well have disastrous results, however carefully it is watered, fed and pruned, as the great majority of those grown in Britain are kinds suited to cultivation out of doors. As a result, the novice may relinquish his interest, concluding that bonsai are too difficult to care for.

Many people do not have gardens in which to grow the more commonly seen species or varieties of bonsai, but this need not deter them from building up a good collection of indoor specimens, provided some thought is given to the kinds chosen for cultivation. Trees hardy in the United Kingdom have, over the centuries, adapted to the eccentricities of climate to the extent that, for example, a period of cold in winter is necessary for their well-being, so the collector of indoor bonsai should turn his attention to trees from warmer climates. Those which are native to the Mediterranean, tropical and desert conditions can, with a little care, be made to grow well on a sunny window-sill. Many of them are accustomed to strong sunlight so careful thought should be given to the positioning of such trees in the home.

Perhaps the best tree to start with indoors is the pomegranate, *Punica granatum* (see Chapter 10). This shrubby tree is endemic from south-eastern Europe to Iran and Afghanistan, but does not require very hot conditions although it appreciates sunshine. Seeds are easy to obtain from the pomegranate fruits which are available in shops early in the year. The numerous seeds should be extracted from the fruit and should then be left to dry for two or three weeks. After planting them in a lime-free, well-drained, peaty, compost mixture it is advisable to water the seed tray with a solution of Cheshunt compound to prevent "damping off". The tray should then be placed in a light position with a bottom heat of about 65° to 70°F (18.5° to 21°C). Germination takes about three weeks and the seedlings, given plenty of light and warmth, grow fast. When they have their second set of true leaves, they can be transplanted for their training to begin. Pomegranates are suited for training to a wide range of sizes and styles. For instance, as mame, or miniature, bonsai (under 6 in [15 cm] in height) the small shiny leaves and fine twiggy structure offer much for the trainer and this, combined with the fast growth rate, can produce an excellent bonsai of this type in two years. For those with more space, desirous of a larger tree, the fast growth and ready response to pruning by branching of the pomegranate will produce a fair-sized, bushy tree in four or five years. To help growth, regular potting on of the tree should be practised, with it being given exposure to

A young pomegranate plant grown from a cutting and showing the results of initial light pruning over a period of four months.

as much sunshine as can possibly be arranged.

The pomegranate will flower from two years of age onwards, provided it is carefully pruned and has access to plenty of sunshine, but initially it is better to concentrate on achieving the size and shape required. Then, once this is established, attempts to get it to flower can be rewarding.

Pomegranates can also be propagated successfully from cuttings of half-ripened shoots taken in July with a heel, and set in peat and sand in a propagating frame heated to a temperature of 60° to 65°F (16° to 18.5°C). Cuttings root readily and can be potted after a few weeks.

The olive family (*Oleaceae*) contains several trees which can easily be trained as bonsai. The olive tree of commerce, *Olea europaea*, can be grown from the seed inside a fresh olive, or from cuttings or suckers when these are obtainable. Like the pomegranate, the olive does not require high temperatures but does appreciate sunshine.

The leaf size of the family varies considerably and, if possible, the smaller-leaved types should be grown. The dark green, silvery-backed foliage is most attractive and, being evergreen, can be enjoyed in the winter months. The trees can be trained as mame bonsai or in various informal upright styles. Those obtained from suckers may offer potential as multiple-trunk bonsai. A soil mixture of loam and leaf-mould with plenty of sand or grit added will suit olives well.

Lemon, lime and grapefruit trees are easy to grow from seeds in pots, although some people may find difficulty in persuading young trees to form a branched structure. This is easily overcome with a combination of pinching out of the leading shoot when the young tree is growing strongly, and cutting off leaves to encourage development of the vestigial buds in the leaf-axils. This will also encourage smaller, finer foliage which, being a shiny, rich green and also evergreen, will enhance the tree throughout the year. Root growth in citrus trees is quite strong and attention to root-pruning will be an additional help in creating the branched structure so essential to the bonsai.

Citrus trees grown indoors can attract one or two undesirable visitors. Scale insects are rather unpleasant and if left to infest a tree can seriously weaken it. Scale can be removed from a bonsai by brushing with cotton wool-wrapped sticks, dipped in paraffin or methylated spirits.

Red spider infestations may also appear. They are more likely in the rather dry air of a house and should be guarded against with all indoor bonsai. The best prevention is to stand all bonsai on a tray of gravel, which can be watered at the same time as the trees, creating a humid microclimate around the trees which the red spider dislikes.

So far, the trees considered have been those accustomed to climates only a little warmer than our own. All these, when trained as bonsai, benefit from spending some weeks or months out of doors during the warmer months of the year. This is not, however, essential.

Among the more exotic varieties that have been trained as bonsai in Britain are some whose seed is not readily obtainable. This need not deter the enthusiast as friends travelling far afield may be able to bring back the necessary seeds for the interest of recreating holiday memories for themselves. One possibility is the mahogany tree, *Swietenia mahogani*, from the West Indies and Southern Florida. This makes an interesting addition to a collection. The seeds, like large-size mahogany-coloured sycamore seeds, develop inside a large lantern-like pod which, when ripe, splits open. High temperatures are needed to germinate the seeds (about 80°F [27°C]), but, once started, the seedlings will happily develop in a lime-free, well-drained compost in a sunny and reasonably warm spot. The foliage, which is pinnate, has a lovely bronze hue when young and the trunk rapidly develops a striated effect.

Guava (*Psidium* species) and coffee (*Coffea arabica*) trees are interesting to grow. The latter are most attractive, with shiny green leaves and a readily branching structure. Initial germination requires considerable warmth (about 80°F [27°C]) but, once growing, normal house temperatures will suffice. Coffee trees have attractive flowers and might bloom after about four years. Guavas vary, seed from yellow and red guavas producing, respectively, light or dark green leaved plants. The growth habit is similar to that of box trees, in that the leaves are opposite (positioned opposite to each other), rather than alternate as in most trees.

From Australia come many members of the acacia family. These have bipinnate leaves and might be considered by many people rather difficult as bonsai. However, many of them can be trained to produce most attractive bonsai specimens, though few will flower unless given more sun than is usual in Britain.

The vast genus *Ficus* (a member of which is the familiar rubber plant, *Ficus elastica*) contains many species suitable for training as indoor bonsai. *Ficus benjamima* is perhaps the most obvious choice, but as it is hard to grow from seed, it is a good idea to purchase a young plant from a florist or garden centre. When allowed to develop as well-grown pot specimens these trees are reminiscent of the weeping birch in habit. However, they are easily trained as bonsai, and can be made to form attractive spreading, informal, upright trees, on which the naturally modest-sized leaves will readily reduce. This ficus does not like low temperatures at any time and should be kept in a place where the temperature does not drop below 65°F (18.5°C). The nearer indoor bonsai can be kept to conditions in which they would most happily grow as full-size trees, the easier their training becomes.

Another interesting ficus is the Moreton Bay fig, *F. macrophylla*, emanating from Australia. It develops, while still very young, a swollen base to its trunk and later on will produce aerial roots. The effect is very unusual and yet the tree is easily grown from seed and undemanding in its care.

Ficus pumila is a small-leaved member of the genus which has a creeping growth habit, spreading and climbing rather like ivy. It can be trained to form a small, interesting bonsai of informal upright shape or is suitable as a cascade-style tree. It is less demanding in its requirements than most ficuses, although it will not tolerate neglect in watering.

Palms will respond to bonsai training. The date palm, *Phoenix dactylifera*, can be grown from the seeds obtained from dates. These will germinate readily in pots of lime-free, sandy soil at a temperature of 75°F (24°C), the first leaf looking like a thickened blade of grass. As the foliage develops divided leaves are produced, eventually becoming true palm leaves. If cultivated in a pot, the date palm shows a strong tendency to produce a root system of a very few, thick, strong tap-roots. It is essential to change this if dwarfing, as opposed to starving, is to occur. The young date palm should have the tip of its first tap-root removed when it has a couple of "leaves", and once-yearly root pruning is essential to develop a more finely divided root system. May is perhaps the best month in which to carry out this task.

Other palms tolerant of house cultivation are *Phoenix canariensis*, the Canary Islands palm, and the Chusan or Chinese fan palm, *Livistona chinensis*, which is on the edge of hardiness in the most favoured parts of Britain, Cornwall particularly. Seeds of these species are not readily available, but young plants may be obtained from florists or garden centres.

Another plant which is superficially palm-like is the cycad, a member of the *Cycadaceae* family. Cycads are strange, primitive plants, in appearance like a cross between a palm and a fern. Many are difficult to grow, but *Cycas revoluta* can be trained as a bonsai in a similar manner to a palm. Growth is erratic, the cycad producing a number of "leaves" simultaneously, which remain on the plant until the next whorl of leaves appears a year or two later. The leaves are trained to weep gracefully by hanging weights on them as they grow.

The root-pruning treatment described for palms (see above) is necessary

"THE SWAMPS"

Taxodium distichum
(swamp cypress)

This tall, elegant group of three large trees has been recently planted and is at the beginning of a period of training designed to improve its unity.

Taxodiums are rarely used for bonsai in Britain, although they are easy to grow, respond well to training, and present far fewer problems in their day-to-day care than many other trees. They tolerate standing for long periods in water, and these three were actually grown for 10 years in flower pots standing in a pond. Over this period they received a minimum of training, pruning being confined to a twice-yearly tidy-up of over-long growth. Then for a year they were more intensely pruned, unwanted branches, especially near the top, being removed completely and the wiring of side branches carried out.

At this stage they were brought to London, to be kept during the winter months in another pond before being substantially root-pruned in order that they could be potted in a very shallow, rectangular Yamaki suiban. This type of container is unsuited to most bonsai because of the lack of drainage holes, although the material of which it is made has some porosity. The trees were potted in early March, and the group was then placed in a greenhouse on heated staging to encourage root development.

Taxodiums break into leaf later than most other trees and at the beginning of May that year foliage appeared and developed. The group was carefully under-planted with dwarf ferns and the soil in the container was landscaped, creating the effect of a lakeside. This acted as a foil to the strongly upright nature of the planting and complemented the fine, feathery foliage. The soil was carefully covered with moss, the "lake" being suggested by a small area of white gravel at the front of the pot.

These taxodiums were exhibited at the Chelsea Flower Show in 1981, and became the group planting of that year. Onlookers were surprised when told their age, for the trunks already had character and the interesting red colour which contrasts so well with the light green of the leaves. Most attractive in autumn when the foliage turns a rich mahogany-red before dropping, the group is known as "The Swamps". The present height is 35 in (88 cm) and the container measures 21 in (52.5 cm) by 14 in (35 cm) by 1½ in (4 cm).

"THE SWAMPS"

Taxodium distichum
(swamp cypress)

"THE SCOTTISH ROCK"

Three *Pinus parviflora*
Planted on Rock

"THE SCOTTISH ROCK"

Three *Pinus parviflora*
Planted on Rock

The piece of rock used in this planting was sent from Japan, arriving broken in many pieces. It was stuck together with high-strength epoxy resin. The pines were young imported trees, whose shapes did not lend themselves to a coventional form of planting, but an exhibit of rock-planted bonsai was staged at the R. H. S. Great Autumn Show in September, 1979 and it was decided to use it. Fixing the hard and heavy rock to the 11 in (28 cm) diameter English tray presented considerable problems as, due to its weight, it was potentially unstable. Eventually flat metal plates were glued to the base, and these were both wired and glued into the container.

The upper and left-hand pines did not have their roots in the soil around the base of the rock but were attached to the back of it and were growing in a mixture of peat and clay, which was prevented from being washed away by a covering of moss. Training wires were attached in crevices in the rock, using lead foil and a centre-punch, and the upper trees carefully wired into position. The right-hand tree was easier to deal with as some of its roots reached the soil in the tray. The trunk was originally attached to the rock to steady it but the wire that did this was subsequently removed. Small branches on all three pines were wired to modify their positions and the soil at the base was sloped up to the rock and covered with moss.

Although the group is not large (the overall height is 21 in or 52.5 cm) the rock has an interesting shape and character. The massiveness of the planting enables it to be successfully placed alongside large individual bonsai of great age without it losing its impact. On such occasions it is positioned to one side of a very shallow oval yamaki tray of the silver-grey colour so beautifully displayed by this pottery. White sand is placed in the tray and sloped gently upwards to cover the English tray, moss being used to emphasise the shadow under the right-hand pine.

Exhibited in such a manner at Chelsea in 1980 and at the Royal Show in 1981, the rock planting is now undergoing further training and development. The pines are aged between 10 and 15 years. To the author it is reminiscent of scenes in the mountains of Scotland, from where her family originated, and it is, therefore, named, perhaps inappropriately, "The Scottish Rock".

This Cycas revoluta, *having undergone limited bonsai training for a four-year period, has developed numerous side growths.*

for cycads as well, and has the added advantage of encouraging them to produce side shoots which will also produce whorls of foliage. This branching will occur quite quickly in a bonsai-trained cycad, although when the plant grows in its natural habitat it may not occur for over 50 years! The cycad is very long-lived and will tolerate (though not appreciate) much neglect. As growing from seed is always slow and usually unsuccessful, the collector is recommended to start by obtaining a young plant.

The genus *Leptospermum*, nearly all of whose members are native to Australia, provides a complete contrast to the palms, cycads and ficuses. Many leptospermums grow naturally like little trees, with very small dark green leaves, a fine twiggy structure, and pretty red or pink flowers in summer. Small plants are sometimes obtainable from specialist shrub and alpine plant nurseries. Intolerant of winter wet, but otherwise nearly hardy in Britain, these make ideal bonsai for the owners of cold conservatories, and when they are container-grown they will, unlike many plants, flower readily. The training is simple, rather akin to pruning a *Zelkova serrata* (see Chapter 6). This is an elm with a twiggy, much branched structure and is readily obtained. Of a similar growth habit, *Baeckea gunniana*, an Australian mountain shrub, can be grown from seed and has the same requirements. The baeckeas are members of the myrtle family.

As can be seen, there are many plants that can be trained as indoor bonsai and which will live for many years given reasonable conditions. The majority of them favour growing in a lime-free compost comprising loam, leaf-mould or peat and plenty of sharp sand or grit. Like house plants, indoor bonsai should be watered with rain-water whenever possible and a supply of this should be kept at room temperature. Tap water should really be avoided and certainly should never be given fresh from the tap. Water for plants should be stored away from light to prevent the formation of algae.

Many indoor bonsai suffer from dryness of the atmosphere. Those trees which come from humid climates should be helped by providing humidity. Such trees can be stood on a shallow tray containing clean gravel or sand, which can be watered at the same time as the trees. Water will evaporate from the sand during the day to provide the necessary humid microclimate around the little trees. It has already been mentioned that this will also help prevent infestations of red spider mite, as will regular spraying with a mist sprayer.

Most indoor bonsai will benefit from annual re-potting, regular feeding with a well-diluted general-purpose liquid fertiliser, and an occasional clear-water "wash" with a spray or fine shower head to keep their foliage fresh and clean. Some varieties grow very fast during the summer months and with these particularly regular pruning or pinching back of growth will show dividends in rapidly creating the shape which leads to an attractive tree.

The enthusiast who wishes to grow hot-climate trees from seed will find this easier if he obtains a small, electrically-heated, thermostatically-controlled propagator. However, with care, results can be obtained using a radiator or boiler as a heat source for germination.

Both indoor and outdoor bonsai, particularly after initial training, look better in shallow containers. As those for indoor work do not need to be frost-proof (although they should be porous, have drainage holes and stand on "feet") they are slightly easier to obtain than the pots for outdoor bonsai, which have almost always to be obtained from a specialist supplier.

One problem arising in the growing of tropical trees is that there is very little literature available to guide the beginner wishing to gain an understanding of their growing conditions in nature. This can, to some extent, be overcome by talking to people familiar with the countries of origin of the trees. Discussing aspects of how they grow naturally, in sun or in shade, in jungles or in deserts or whether they are tall or small, can provide useful information as a guide to cultivation. Such contacts may also provide additional sources of seeds and are, therefore, of especial interest to the collector of indoor bonsai.

CHAPTER SIX

TRAINING

The training given to a bonsai is often the subject of uninformed criticism. The techniques used, either in the shaping of a young tree to appear old and artistic, in the "improving" of a tree grown in the wild to correct nature's defects and enhance suitable features, or in the maintenance of both, are all adaptations of principles used for centuries in gardening around the world.

To give examples of the way in which traditional gardening methods have been adapted to the training and cultivation of bonsai, one need only consider "wiring", which is often described by critics of bonsai as the torturing of trees by binding them with wire and bending them into strange positions. But a walk around the kitchen garden of almost any of the stately homes of Britain will be enough to reveal some fine examples of fan-trained peach trees, espalier-trained apple trees and grape vines in greenhouses which are growing neatly in a criss-cross grid. It has been the custom to train these trees by tying suitable branches to wires which are supported by posts, or attached to a wall. After a period, the branches will stay in the positions in which they have been tied, and winding wire around a bonsai branch to hold it in position is simply a free-standing method of doing the same thing. It has exactly the same effect.

Or again, bonsai trainers may be accused of "cutting off everything as fast as it will grow" by those people who, when in their own gardens, take a pride in cutting their lawns regularly, maintaining their privet hedges at a certain well-defined height, and annually cutting their roses back to a few short stubby twigs. Bonsai trees are not formed into artificial images of birds and animals, as in topiary, nor are they starved of nourishment, although old bonsai specimens originally coming from the wild may superficially have that appearance due to the rugged nature of their trunks. They are healthily growing, long-lived trees which are simply maintained at a small size in a small container and which give an infinite amount of pleasure to those who tend and care for them. However, it is not possible to over-simplify the process of training. Each stage is easy enough, but it is a combination of all the parts that create the natural-looking, dwarfed, containerized tree in an artificial environment.

Most readers will be interested primarily in training their own trees from young stock. Sources of material can range from purpose-grown seedlings, young wild trees or rooted cuttings, to happy "accidents" found in garden centres. The aspiring collector should feel some sympathy with his intended bonsai, an interest in its shape and anticipated development and, importantly, he should have more than one such young tree. To the novice and experienced collector alike, there is a feeling of frustration in waiting for one tree to grow that seems to disappear when the interest is spread over five or 10 or more trees. The skill in training them also increases rapidly when working on several trees, so that individual ones become pleasing to look at in a shorter time, providing an inspiration for their trainer.

Before explaining in greater detail the techniques used to train and maintain bonsai trees, it is pehaps worth pausing for a moment to consider whether there are reasons, other than the dictates of Japanese fashion and tradition, why bonsai are shaped the way they are. The earlier Japanese collectors had little help from horticultural science and evolved their methods by a combination of inherited knowledge and trial and error. An accumulation of experience over many years taught them the limitations of their craft and enabled trees to be trained as quickly as possible in the manner best suited to the species. Practical possibilities thus combined and produced an aesthetically pleasing result.

Two features of the well-trained and mature bonsai, regardless of the style in which it is trained, are firstly the comparatively wide spacing between individual branches which necessitates the creation of an attractive effect with comparatively few of them. Secondly, despite these branches spreading in all directions, they have very little thickness, the foliage springing directly from old and young wood, and almost every leaf showing itself. The resulting overall appearance is perhaps reminiscent of, and as impressive as, an old and stately cedar of Lebanon in a parkland setting. It is interesting to learn from recent research in plant physiology that the traditional styles into which bonsai are trained are not only aesthetically pleasing but allow the bonsai to function very efficiently as a living plant.

Many people are aware that any green plant is able to live and grow because of the process known as photosynthesis, the ability of the leaves to manufacture glucose and other complex organic substances used in cell production, from carbon dioxide, water and the sun's energy. Although the efficiency of leaves to undertake this process is affected by a number of different factors, such as carbon dioxide concentration, wind speed and so on, the most important factor relating to efficiency is light. Put simply, a leaf can photosynthesise most efficiently in full light and, if shaded, its efficiency is reduced. Should a leaf be shaded by four or five other leaves it can no longer photosynthesise. It does not, however, do nothing, for it is in fact respiring. That is, it is using its own organic compounds to produce carbon dioxide and water vapour, which it releases into the atmosphere. During hours of darkness all leaves are respiring, but when this process is carried on by a proportion of foliage during the day, it is putting a considerable burden on the plant. Thus the training of a bonsai branch to be wide-spreading yet of little thickness, and the wide spacing of the branches which allow light to reach the lower foliage as well as the upper branches, can be seen to be beneficial to the tree in its efficient functioning.

A young tree will, if left unpruned, grow upwards for some years at the expense of lateral branching. A young tree undergoing bonsai training behaves somewhat differently if regularly pruned. It develops lateral branches and these then further divide to create a multitude of twiggy growth. As the tree matures, the tendency for it to produce a multitude of growth at the crown diminishes, and it is spread more evenly over all the branches.

It is known that apical buds contain a substance (Indole-3-acetic acid) which inhibits the development of lateral buds. At the same time plant nutrients are attracted to the growing apical shoot at the expense of other areas. When the apical shoot is removed by pruning, a diversion of the inhibiting substance allows lateral shoots to develop and plant nutrients are attracted to those areas. Regular pruning reduces apical dominance, encouraging the growth of lateral shoots to create a finely-divided twiggy structure.

Because research in plants is mainly concentrated on those kinds which produce crops of economic importance, little work appears to have been carried out on the effect of root pruning on ornamental plants. Observation, however, shows that a plant makes considerable lateral root growth when the tap root is removed. It can also be shown that when a tree has 25 per cent of its root system removed, it responds by producing much shorter, more compact growth, although the reasons for this are not fully understood. At present the bonsai collector must content himself with the knowledge gained over centuries and accept that his trees will live happily for many years dwarfed by pruning and root-pruning as necessary, and that this will contribute much towards a long and healthy life.

THE TOOLS NEEDED

The novice bonsai owner may feel ill-equiped to start pruning and wiring his young trees. Most Western garden tools are designed for use on large shrubs, roses and so on and appear too big and unwieldy for a tiny bonsai. There is a wide range of suitable ones which are specially made in Japan for use on bonsai trees, but few of these are seen in Britain, and interest by and large is confined to two or three of the most useful imported items. These are extremely well made and therefore expensive to buy, a problem aggravated by their weight, which makes them costly to bring half way round the world, added to which there are various duties and taxes as well.

In the following pages a number of these tools will be described and, where practical, more readily available British substitutes will be suggested. But before turning to these it is worth considering whether you have space to install a table or workbench. If this can be done, extra shelves for the tools can be put up at the same time, and it will all be very worthwhile.

The turntable One of the most useful tools is a turntable. Those from Japan are supplied with a brake, so that the bonsai may be revolved and then held steady. They have a top measuring about 1ft by 1ft (30 cm by 30 cm) and will safely support extremely large, heavy bonsai. As a substitute, a cake-icing turntable will suffice for most trees that the amateur collector is likely to own, and it may be possible to fit a braking mechanism.

Scissors These are an important part of the bonsai trainer's tool-kit. There

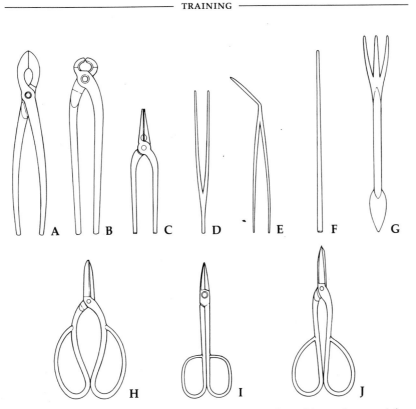

A. *Side branch cutters.* **B.** *Wire cutters.* **C.** *Jinning tool.* **D.** *Pincers (tweezers) for removing dead leaves.* **E.** *Tweezers with trowel end.* **F.** *Chopstick.* **G.** *Rake with spatula.* **H.** *Scissors for cutting fine roots.* **I.** *Scissors for cutting fine twiggy growth and* **J.** *Scissors for cutting shoots.*

are different grades of scissors for leaf-pruning (deciduous trees other than flowering varieties), for trimming·and pruning thin twigs, for pruning fibrous roots protruding from the soil after re-potting and for cutting the thin grades of wire. The scissors are all long-handled to facilitate pruning otherwise inaccessible twigs. Further pairs of scissors are available for branch pruning or root pruning.

Side branch cutters These are available in two or three sizes and designs and are perhaps the most useful of all the Japanese tools. There is no effective substitute that will, in one operation, remove a branch flush with the trunk, leaving a slight hollow to enable the bark to grow over and leave the trunk smooth. The same effect can be achieved, however, by using wood carving tools to make the hollow after cutting the branch as close as possible to the trunk.

Root pruners These are a larger version of the above and are intended for cutting large roots. They leave a flat rather than a curved surface and are strong powerful tools, but a really good pair of secateurs or branch loppers should be able to cope with most roots.

Jinning tool This is like a pair of round-ended pliers and is used for creating jins (see Chapter 7). An ordinary pair of pliers can be used for this job and, bearing in mind that jinning should be done sparingly, this is a less essential tool.

Carving tools and knives These may be used in conjunction with the jinning tool in the creation of "dead wood" effects, and also when large branches are removed and areas around the wound carved to make the bonsai appear naturally split in various ways. Woodworking shops carry a wide range of such tools and a set to suit individual needs can be easily bought. An oilstone to keep them sharp is an essential extra item.

Some Japanese knives are designed specifically for grafting purposes, but British made ones are of similar high quality.

Pincers One useful piece of equipment is a pair of pincers (tweezers). This has many uses, including removing dead leaves from among twiggy growth. The specially made Japanese examples are noticeably long-handled with curved tips and, as a bonus, a spatulate end for pressing down soil. The best place to find good pincers is at a medical/surgical equipment supplier. They are very useful in day-to-day bonsai care.

Chopsticks These are perhaps the most used of all tools at potting time. A short, fine one is useful when potting mame bonsai, and a regular size of chopstick is useful for most other trees. Widely available in many qualitities ("cooking" quality is quite adequate) they are cheap and essential to the bonsai collector. And while on the subject of potting, other tools are used for this in Japan. For instance, sieves are used to grade soil. These are obtainable in various qualities and mesh sizes, one of ¼ in (.5 cm) mesh size being perhaps most used. Trowels are also needed, both the normal garden size and the smaller sizes marketed for pot plants.

Plastic mesh netting Holes in pots need to be covered in order to prevent soil falling out and worms from entering. Potsherds may be useful, though the pieces will take up more room than is desirable, especially in a small pot. Some collectors use perforated zinc, but drainage with this is not as good as needed, especially when the zinc becomes old and oxydised. The best solution is plastic mesh netting. This is light, easy to obtain and re-useable.

Other tools Other tools used from time to time will all be found in good tool shops. Various sizes of saw (with teeth for cross-cutting), are used for removing large branches. Hammers, chisels and centre-punches are all used in rock-planting bonsai work. A watering can with a very fine spray nozzle, especially for watering newly-potted bonsai, is not as easy to locate as one might think, but can be obtained. The Japanese produce a very fine and well-designed nozzle for use with hosepipes, but unfortunately this does not fit commonly-used British hose sizes. Sprayers are useful for misting foliage and for the application of insecticides.

Copper wire Copper wire of various thicknesses will be required for bending branches, and also plastic-coated wire for use with bonsai specimens having sensitive bark.

A jack If large branches or trunks are to be bent the Japanese use a tool known as a jack. This consists of a rectangular metal plate, through which are screwed at either end two hook-shaped pieces of metal and between them, also screwed through it, a flat-ended piece of metal. This is used as a pivot, the hooks pulling on either side to bend a branch at a given point. The whole thing is fully adjustable. A tool of this sort could be made in Britain by anyone with a penchant for metalwork. It is very useful when working on larger trees.

Tool maintenance If an area of a house or shed can be set aside for bonsai working, most of these tools may be kept to hand in one place. All cutting tools should be cleaned after use and lightly oiled to ensure a long working life. Japanese cutting tools are not stainless, so especial care should be taken to keep them free from rust, particularly in view of the difficulty and expense in obtaining them. Always buy the best-possible quality tools as these will give better service for a far longer time than the cheaper alternatives one might be tempted to buy.

WIRING

The wiring of bonsai trunks and branches into desired shapes is a comparatively modern method of training that allows for greater freedom of style than long-term pruning and tying alone.

The preferred wire for bonsai is copper, made softer by gentle heating in a low temperature fire. When cool, it can then easily be wound round a trunk or branch, its pliability helping prevent damage to the bark. When the branch has been bent to the required position and an appropriate thickness of softened wire applied to hold it, the latter will harden and continue to hold the branch until it is set in position. Trees to be used should be healthy and established in their containers. Weak or sick trees should not be used, nor should newly potted trees or those immediately due to be re-potted, as the additional stress of wiring could kill them. Bending a branch stretches the water vessels on the outer perimeter of the curve. Over a period of time these adjust to the new position, but indecision, resulting in bending a branch many different ways, can have the effect of ring-barking, which will also kill it.

The length of the wire will need to be about twice the length of the branch. It must, of course, be fixed at one end and this is usually done by first winding it round the trunk just below the branch. It is then wound around

(Continued on p. 82)

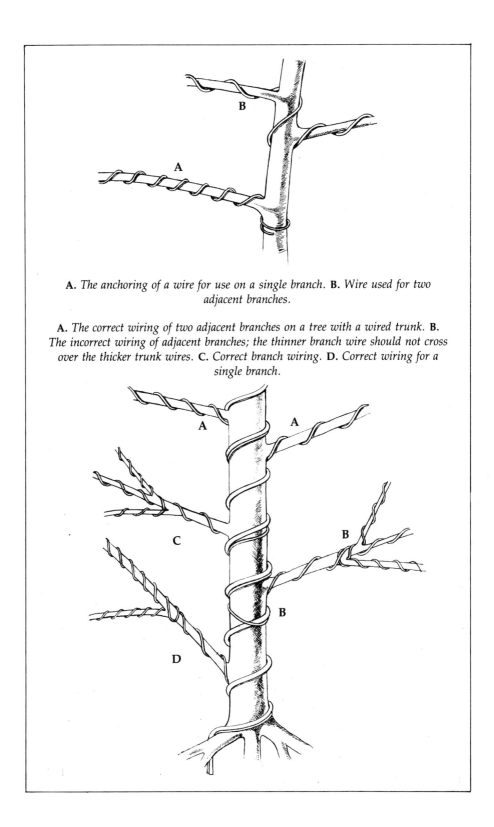

A. *The anchoring of a wire for use on a single branch.* **B.** *Wire used for two adjacent branches.*

A. *The correct wiring of two adjacent branches on a tree with a wired trunk.* **B.** *The incorrect wiring of adjacent branches; the thinner branch wire should not cross over the thicker trunk wires.* **C.** *Correct branch wiring.* **D.** *Correct wiring for a single branch.*

LEFT: *An aged* Pinus thunbergii *which has been kept in the shade for nine years. During this period its training wires were not removed, nor was it re-potted or pruned. Neglected training wires have cut deeply into the bark, causing considerable disfigurement.*

BELOW: *The same tree during re-positioning and with some preliminary work having been carried out.*

the branch itself in the direction in which it is to be bent from the thicker to the thinner end, not so tightly that it presses into and bruises the bark, nor so loosely that there are gaps between the wire and bark. The branch must be held steady throughout the process.

The wire should, when completely coiled around the branch, be neat and tidy with each coil equally spaced. A branch of about the thickness of a pencil will generally need one turn of wire per ¼ in (.5 cm) along its length. Should the wire not be strong enough, two pieces may be used. They should be wound in the same direction and be close to one another, rather than in a criss-cross fashion. Once wired, the branch should be bent carefully into the desired position. The best way to learn the correct tension and spacing between the coils of wire is to try it on free-growing shrubs or trees in the garden. Experience will show the thicknesses and lengths of wire required, varying with the plant in question, and also the times of year it is best to avoid when there is a temporary brittleness of the branches. Some kinds resent metal wire on their bark, notably *Prunus* and *Cryptomeria*. For these trees, paper-wrapped or plastic-coated wire may be used.

Wiring is often used to create a basic shape for a bonsai with spreading branches which are parallel to the ground, rather than for the more typical, nearly-vertical branch positions of many young trees. It is of interest to note that branches in the horizontal position elongate less than upright ones and have a shorter distance between joints. Also, probably due to the distribution of chemicals within the branch, more fruiting spurs are developed, which is of advantage when training varieties for flowering bonsai such as prunus, malus and so on.

BONSAI STYLES

A bonsai can be described as having a particular style according to its growth and training. Within each style there is individual variation between one tree and another.

FORMAL UPRIGHT (Chokkan) Trees trained in this way should have straight, tapering trunks and well-spaced branches radiating from the trunk and parallel to the soil. It is not often seen in Britain, due, perhaps, to the rarity of young trees growing in nurseries suitable for this style of training. Trees most often seen as chokkan bonsai include *Cryptomeria japonica*, *Pinus parviflora* and *P. thunbergii*.

INFORMAL UPRIGHT (Moyogi) This style covers a range into which the majority of bonsai can be classified. It varies from the "pine style" with one or two well-balanced curves in the trunk, to the "natural looking" maple or hornbeam.

TWIN TRUNK (Sokan) Whether or not a sokan bonsai appears credible will depend on the relative thicknesses of the "mother" and "child" trunks, which have a common root. Similar bonsai may have three trunks (sankan) or five trunks (gokan). Trees are rarely trained having four trunks, this being a number difficult to balance visually.

SLANTING (Shakan) These bonsai are very popular with the novice, who sometimes pots a tall tree at an angle in an effort to reduce its height. The true shakan bonsai, however, should appear balanced and have branches growing on either side of the trunk.

WINDSWEPT (Fukinagashi) Although there may be a superficial similarity to the shakan bonsai, "windswept" trees are characterised by their branches arising from one side of the trunk only and sweeping in one direction.

MULTIPLE TRUNK (Kabudachi) These bonsai have numerous trunks arising from a single root, in the manner of a suckering elm or prunus. They can be mistaken for the next style, ikada. A variant of the kabudachi bonsai is the setsurassari where the trunks arise from a more sinuous root.

RAFT (Ikada) Where a bonsai has the majority of its branches on one side of the trunk, an ikada can be created by lying it horizontally on the soil and training the branches to be trunks. In time, new roots will grow from the original trunk and the old root-ball can be removed.

BROOM (Hokidachi) These bonsai are so named because they resemble an up-turned, old-fashioned birch broom. Some have all their branches radiating from the trunk at a single point, while others have a similar silhouette but the trunk tapers evenly to the tip of the tree, the branches radiating in a tapering sequence of length and thickness from about one-third of the overall height upwards. Almost all specimens of hokidachi bonsai are of the elm-like *Zelkova serrata*.

CASCADE (Kengai) As its Western name implies, the branches of the kengai bonsai flow over the side of the pot, giving the effect of a waterfall. These bonsai are usually potted in a deep pot, to give balance, and are raised up for display purposes as the branches may cascade some distance below the base of the container.

SEMI-CASCADE (Han kengai) Rather similar to an extreme form of shakan bonsai, the han kengai bonsai has its branches ending below the rim of the pot (which is usually of some depth) but not below the base.

LITERATI (Bunjingi) This style evolved from the cultural movement known as Nanga, followed by painters of the Southern school of Chinese landscape painting. These artists were also scholars of religion, philosophy and the arts who, stifled by the formalities surrounding their lives, became contempla-tives. Their paintings of trees showed the freedom for which they were searching, with elongated trunks apparently wandering at will, and with a few strangely-positioned branches giving the whole an exciting appearance, somewhat reminiscent, to the western mind, of oriental caligraphy.

(*Continued on p. 92*)

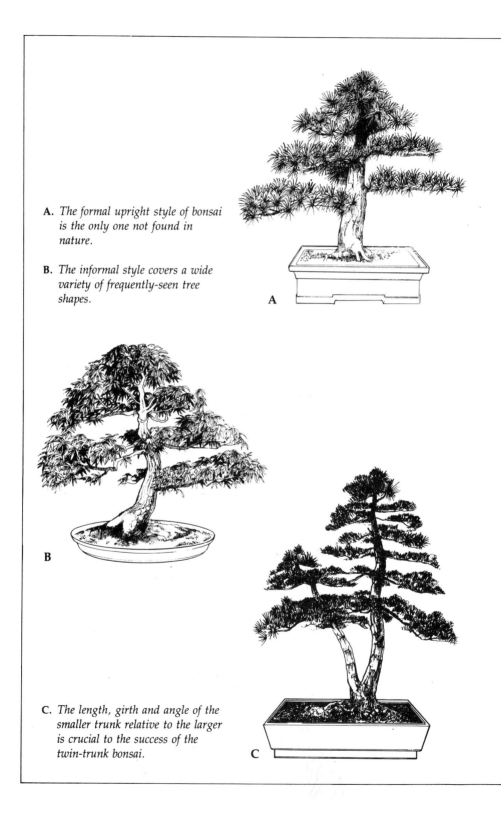

A. The formal upright style of bonsai is the only one not found in nature.

B. The informal style covers a wide variety of frequently-seen tree shapes.

A

B

C. The length, girth and angle of the smaller trunk relative to the larger is crucial to the success of the twin-trunk bonsai.

C

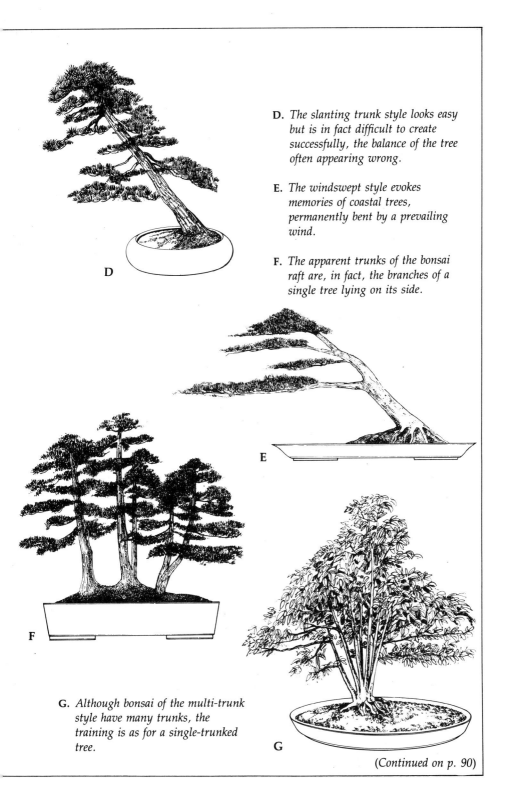

D. *The slanting trunk style looks easy but is in fact difficult to create successfully, the balance of the tree often appearing wrong.*

E. *The windswept style evokes memories of coastal trees, permanently bent by a prevailing wind.*

F. *The apparent trunks of the bonsai raft are, in fact, the branches of a single tree lying on its side.*

D

E

F

G. *Although bonsai of the multi-trunk style have many trunks, the training is as for a single-trunked tree.*

G

(Continued on p. 90)

"THE MAPLE"

Acer palmatum 'Chisio'
(Japanese red maple)

This very fine old bonsai is a joy to behold in spring when, for several weeks, its young leaves and developing shoots are a clear cerise-red. It was imported into Britain in 1969 for a private collector, who trained it carefully for several years before it passed into another collection. After a time it became neglected due to the frequent absence of the owner, and a few years ago found its way into the author's collection.

Some dead branches were found to have been removed and others were dying, added to which there was a very severe infestation of scale insect which, if left untended, would have killed it. The insects were removed by hand, red maples reacting adversely to any form of insecticidal spray. Stumps of dead branches were removed and considerable amounts of dead twiggy growth trimmed off.

This bonsai, unlike most others, has to the present time a recorded history of 144 years, and was cared for by three generations of a Japanese family for 71 of them. To have allowed such a tree to die would have been to lose a slice of history, and fortunately it is now healthy and well.

Formerly potted in the container now housing the author's "Big Crab" it was re-potted four or five years ago into its present container, a white, glazed, shallow, oval container, 25 in (62.5 cm) by 18 in (45 cm) by 2¾ in (7 cm), which enhances the elegant curve at the base of its wide trunk. The present girth is 11½ in or 29 cm.

The tree's silhouette is now being modified in easy stages with selective pruning to give it better balance. The right-hand side should be wider as it is from there that the lower branch comes.

This bonsai is unusual, not only because of its size, age and quality but also for the fact that it appears to be growing on its own roots. Recent imports of lesser specimens of *Acer palmatum* 'Chisio' from Japan have always been grafted plants and this kind is notoriously difficult to root, cuttings being unlikely to survive their first winter. It is a magnificent specimen, enhanced each spring by its uniquely-coloured foliage and giving a reminder of the glory when, for a few brief days in autumn, it turns again to a striking colour. In respect for its quality it is named simply "The Maple".

"THE MAPLE"

Acer palmatum 'Chisio'
(Japanese red maple)

"ANNE'S PINE"

Pinus parviflora
(Japanese white pine)

"ANNE'S PINE"

Pinus parviflora
(Japanese white pine)

This classically-shaped Japanese white pine bonsai was imported in 1978, together with two others, in order to fill a gap in the author's collection. Such mature examples are hard to come by and, although in 1978 it was badly in need of re-wiring to correct some three or four years of neglect, it was nevertheless a very fine tree. It was also well suited, both in maturity, size and style, to a very fine "pine" pot from the Yamaki pottery, which had been purchased some six months previously in the hope that one day something worthy of such a container could be obtained.

When re-wired, the tree increased in width and each layer of foliage became more distinct, giving immediate improvement to the somewhat hedgehog-like appearance that it had had at the time of purchase. This improvement was even more noticeable in the following year when, in late spring, the new season's "candles" began to develop and grow. Further training will be aimed at increasing the size of the crown, particularly on the right-hand side, and in improving the balance of the branches. This is gradually being achieved, mainly by annual wiring in the late autumn after the summer needle-drop, which is common to all pines.

This pine is remarkably heavy and for this reason is exhibited rarely, the other two imported at the same time being more frequently used, along with lesser specimens. The weight is in no small way due to the potting mixture which is used. Being an old pine (over 100 years old) it has less need than a younger, more vigorously growing tree of rich soil, and was potted in a mixture of 60 per cent sharp grit, 10 per cent loam and 30 per cent pine leaf-mould. It is fed with well-diluted tomato fertiliser in early spring, and again in August and September. It spends much of the summer at high altitude on the North Weald in full sun, this helping to keep its needles short and its colour good.

Currently 33 in (83 cm) in height and with a trunk girth of some 13 in (32.5 cm), the fine silver-grey container measures 18 in (45 cm) by 15 in (38 cm) by 5½ in (14 cm). It is likely to remain in its present pot for many years. It is simply known as "Anne's Pine".

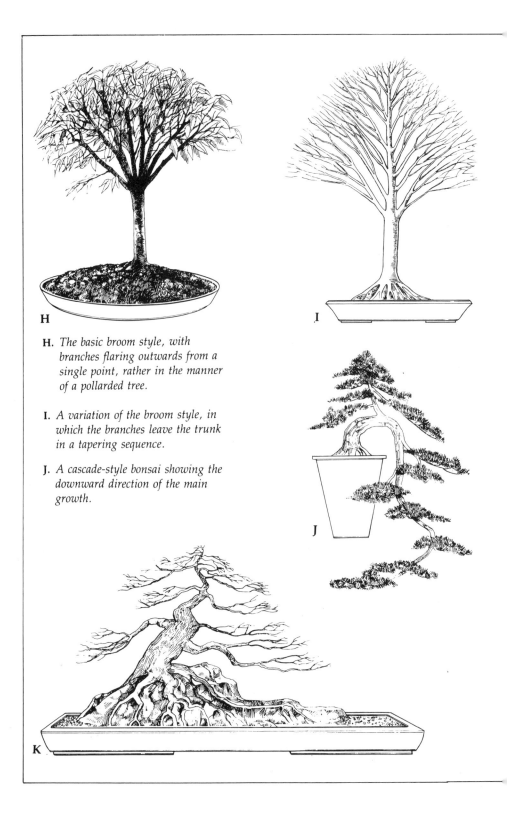

H. The basic broom style, with branches flaring outwards from a single point, rather in the manner of a pollarded tree.

I. A variation of the broom style, in which the branches leave the trunk in a tapering sequence.

J. A cascade-style bonsai showing the downward direction of the main growth.

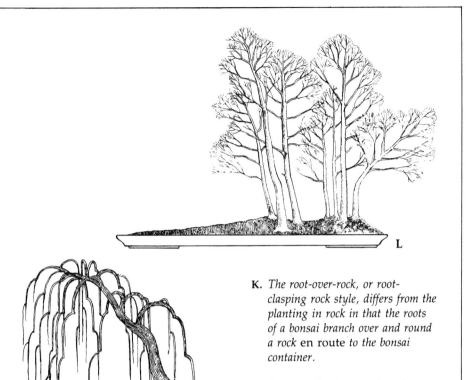

L

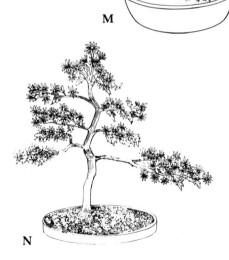

M

N

K. *The root-over-rock, or root-clasping rock style, differs from the planting in rock in that the roots of a bonsai branch over and round a rock en route to the bonsai container.*

L. *A group planting consists of many trees planted to create the effect of a woodland.*

M. *Trees with weeping branches are usually trained in upright or sloping-trunk styles.*

N. *A chrysanthemum trained in the traditional bonsai style. The shape must be established while the plant is young.*

GROUP PLANTING (Yose-ue) As the name implies, a group of trees, usually of the same species, planted to represent a woodland, a spinney, or a grove. Occasionally, deciduous or coniferous trees are mixed, and if successfully done the result can be very striking.

ROCK GROWN (Ishitsuki) This type of planting is seen in two forms.

(a) Trees actually planted on to a rock to create the appearance of a rocky or mountainous terrain. The trees or shrubs used grow into or on to the rock, which for display is generally placed into a shallow tray containing gravel or water.

(b) A tree is trained so that its roots grow over the rock and into the soil in the pot below. The best examples should appear to clasp the rock firmly and roots should be broad and strong. The most commonly seen examples are of *Acer buergeranum*.

WEEPING BRANCH STYLE (Shidare-zukuri) This is not a style on its own, but is the name given to a tree of weeping habit, such as a willow, trained in informal upright, sloping trunk or other styles. Almost exclusively used for willow (*Salix babylonica*) and tamarix, the training differs from most other styles in that the majority of side shoots are retained when growing from the upper surface of the branches, and then encouraged to weep downwards creating a pleasing effect.

MINIATURE BONSAI (Mame) The miniature bonsai, though trained in a number of different styles, are an important category of potted trees which must be approached slightly differently from the larger forms.

In Britain, a mame bonsai of whatever style should be under 6 in (15 cm) in height (7 in [18 cm] in the USA) and in a tiny container. In all other aspects it should have the appearance of a normal-sized bonsai. There are many people who train the dwarf forms of conifers as mame bonsai but as a number of these lose the "tree-like" characteristics of the species and are merely very compact they are not really suitable for the purpose. Small-leaved cultivars of normal-sized trees are ideal for training in this way and though the techniques for shaping larger bonsai are used to create mame, their application is somewhat different.

PERENNIAL CHRYSANTHEMUMS Chrysanthemums may be trained to conform to many of the bonsai styles, flowering annually and creating an interesting and colourful feature in a collection during the late summer and autumn months. Small-leaved and small-flowered varieties may be used and their cultivation and training is somewhat different to bonsai created from forest trees.

CASCADE CHRYSANTHEMUMS (Kengai-giku) Although not strictly true bonsai, as these plants are grown and trained in a single year, they have been cultivated since the start of the century and are grown and shaped with great skill into a variety of cascading shapes. These were first exhibited in Britain in November, 1930 by Mr H Woolman at the Chrysanthemum Society

Exhibition and at the Royal Horticultural Society's New Hall, arousing much interest and admiration. M Vilmorin and M Andrieux a few years later showed such plants at French shows and they were also cultivated in Utrecht by Mr Budde of the Botanic Gardens there. Two recent exhibits at the Royal Horticultural Society shows staged by a local borough indicate that there is still great interest in this unusual skill.

TRAINING TECHNIQUES

The informal upright style The easiest style of bonsai for the beginner to create is the informal upright style or moyogi of the "natural"-looking type. This differs from the chokkan formal upright, in that the guidelines for the latter can be less rigidly applied to give a pleasing result.

The selected tree should have a vertical trunk. It should be turned around and studied from all sides. If it is too tall, its height can be reduced by cutting off the top immediately behind a forward pointing branch, which can then be wired straight up. The finished effect should produce a tree whose trunk has an even taper from base to apex, and this latter should be vertically above the centre of the base of the trunk.

The first branch (the lowest) is very important, being the longest and thickest branch on the tree. It should be either on the right or left of the trunk but never at the front or back. It is usually one-third of the way up the trunk. The second branch should be on the opposite side of the trunk to the first branch and above it. It will be slightly thinner and shorter than the first branch. The third branch should be opposite the second branch and again slightly smaller. Between branches one, two and three are back branches which should point to the rear of the tree but slightly to the left or right in order that they can be seen. They should be shorter in length than the side branches and decrease in diameter as one moves up the trunk. Forward-growing branches are acceptable above eye-level, but like the rear branches they should be pointing slightly to the right or left and never straight forward. They should alternate to the apex. Bonsai are normally trained to be viewed with eye level being roughly one-half to two-thirds of the way up the trunk so that forward pointing branches are acceptable in the upper one-third.

Where a young tree has too many branches, the beginner may be tempted to remove all those not correctly positioned, but it would be better to retain most of them for a while. Their presence will help the trunk to develop in girth. The only branches that must be removed early in a tree's training are thick, coarse upper branches, totally out of proportion, and branches growing directly forwards (eye-poking branches). The latter should be removed while still small, to minimise visiable scarring of the bark of the trunk.

Spacing between selected branches should decrease as the branches become thinner and smaller. This will give the effect of a well-balanced, nicely proportioned tree. The angle selected for them will affect the final appearance of the tree. In general, all branches on a bonsai slope at the same angle, be it downward, horizontal or upward. Exceptionally, some trees have down-

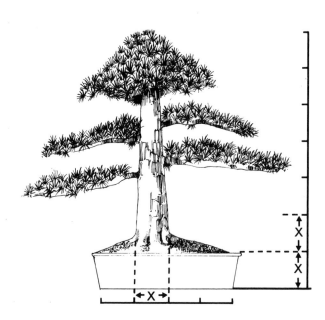

The correct proportions for a bonsai tree in relation to its container.

ward sloping lower branches gradually changing as one moves up the trunk to horizontal and finally, at the apex, pointing upwards, giving the effect of a young, vigorously growing specimen.

The cascade form of training When the collector has successfully created a number of trees in the informal upright style, he is usually keen to try his hand at creating a contrasting style. The cascade form of training offers something completely different. The starting material may be a young, rather leggy tree with a flexible trunk, or an older tree that, although its normal growth habit is upright, through unusual circumstances has grown in the wrong direction. Older trees of this sort may be found on hillsides where an earth-slip may have caused them to be dislodged from their hold and tip over. Surviving this trauma, the trees have continued to grow but in strange and often attractive shapes.

A regular source of potential cascade bonsai material may be obtained from garden centres. Container-grown young trees or shrubs may get knocked over from time to time. Occasionally such plants are overlooked for a considerable period, by which time they have grown into a decidedly bent shape, which may possibly be well-suited to adaptation for a cascade bonsai.

Having selected the starting material, it should be potted in a round, deep pot. Flower pots may be used at this stage, the size depending on the size of the tree. A pot a little on the large size can be advantageous, as trees in the cascade position are slower growing than those in upright training. The flower pots known as "long Toms" are ideal.

A close-up showing details of the wiring of a nursery-grown Acer palmatum, *trained in the cascade style.*

The positioning of the potted cascade bonsai should be considered carefuly. As the tree hangs over the edge of the pot, this cannot be placed on the ground or on an ordinary table. On the edge of a shelf it may be liable to be accidentally knocked off, and during the creative training period at least it is not easy to turn the tree around. Perhaps the thing to use is a structure like a bird table with some form of adequate anchorage for a tall pot.

The tree, once established in its pot, is ready for its training, whether this involves complete wiring and shaping, or perhaps less work due to its convenient shape to begin with.

The formal cascade has an apex created from a suitable branch near the base of the trunk. Growing upward, this forms a crown to the cascade bonsai, while the main trunk continues over the side of the pot, generally moving somewhat away from it before turning in again, so that the final foliage at the tip of the cascade is veritically below the apex. A vertical line downwards from apex to tip should, when viewed from the front, appear to pass through the centre of the base of the trunk and the middle of the top and bottom of the pot.

The slope of branches on the crown and cascade should be similar and generally gently downwards, and the pattern of branching should be similar to that of upright trees. It is acceptable, however, on the cascading section for a proportion of the foliage of the side branches to cross in front of the trunk.

Despite what has just been said, a tree does not necessarily need to have

A Juniperus chinensis *imported from Japan in 1961 and now about 90 years old is trained in the semi-cascade style. It is potted into a deep, square Yamaki pot, ideally suited to this shape of bonsai.*

a crown formed from a suitable branch to be right for cascade-style training. A vertical cascade may be created having no crown, the trunk leading over the edge of the pot to an almost vertical drop, which may or may not turn somewhat upwards at the base.

The semi-cascade style A tree with a crown and rather short but cascade-type trunk can be trained as a semi-cascade. In this style, the trunk rather than dropping vertically over the side of the pot tends to follow the downward-sweeping line of the crown branches, its tip being above the bottom of the pot and well to the side of it. Semi-cascade bonsai are not usually in such deep pots as cascade bonsai and, because their tip is not below the base of the pot, can be stood on a shelf or table for viewing and training.

The waterfall cascade Another variant of the cascade is the waterfall cascade. As its name implies, this style gives the effect of a waterfall, and is created by training a tree with a very short trunk from which arise a number of more or less equal leaders. These are all trained vertically downwards and a branching structure planned by regarding all the cascading leaders as a single unit and selecting suitable side branches for training wherever they might arise. Bonsai of this style can be quite dramatic and a very long waterfall cascade can be an especially rewarding sight for its trainer.

Group planting The novice bonsai trainer may try to grow some of his stock from seed. Of the resulting seedlings, a few will grow in a manner that suggests a particular style for training. Others, whose future does not appear so obvious, can be left quietly growing in training pots, occasionally trimmed to prevent excessive growth but otherwise little worked upon. A group of trees such as these presents the ideal opportunity for the collector to attempt a group planting of bonsai. This can consist of as few as three trees together, or up to 30 or more in a single container. Where there are no more than about 15 it is good practice to avoid even numbers. With more trees, to create a spinney-like effect, this is less important.

Groups of trees trained as bonsai are always potted in a very shallow container, usually termed a tray. Sometimes such groups are seen planted on to a flat piece of slate which, if selected to create a balanced effect with the trees, can look very impressive indeed. In such a planting, the slate is treated as though it were a pot. To form "edges", clay (ordinary), moss peat and water are blended together to form a sticky mixture. This is then applied to the slate at the proposed limits of the planting. It should be pressed into the slate as much as possible, then contoured so that at the sides nearest the edges of the slate the mixture slopes to merge with the slate, the other side being roughly vertical to retain soil. Planting is effected in the normal manner and, when complete, soil and the clay mixture should be covered with moss, which may initially be secured with V-shaped wires.

It is not usually necessary to drill drainage holes in containers of slate or sandstone.

Although groups with two or more mixed kinds of tree can be grown, this is very difficult to do successfully, and the beginner would be advised to construct his first few groups using the same kind. Certain ones lend themselves to group plantings, notably *Zelkova serrata*, Japanese or English beech (*Fagus crenata* and *sylvatica* respectively), maples (*Acer*) among the deciduous trees, and pine, juniper, larch and cryptomeria among the conifers. Seedlings of many species can show considerable variation in leaf size, colour and shape, and care during selection will ensure a grouping of very similar ones. However, the seedlings, although matching well in other respects, should be of differing sizes. In assembling a group planting, the trainer is creating a forest rather than a line of vertical trees.

The focal point of the group should not be centrally placed in the tray, but be to the left or right of centre and behind a centre line across the tray. Perspective is important because, in the space of a few inches, a feeling of great depth has to be created. This is achieved by placing the tallest tree (which should also have the thickest trunk) at the front, middle-sized trees part-way back and the smallest trees (with the thinnest trunks) at the rear. However, if a number of trees are used, it is generally more effective to group the larger ones together near one side of the tray, and to have smaller trees forming another group more centrally placed but with empty space between them and also on the other side of the tray. Very small trees can be used in the rear to give the effect of distance. Trees on the edge of the group

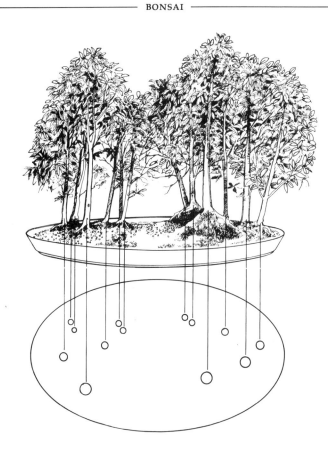

*Plan and elevation views of a group planting of bonsai. Note that those trees with
the thickest trunks should be the tallest and nearest to the front of the group.*

can lean slightly outwards, their outer branches reaching into the space. This
gives a feeling of reality, as full-sized trees in forests reach out and grow
towards the light.

The planting of a group may take some time, due to the complications of
holding each tree in the correct position and the fact that there is little space
between them for movements of the hands. However, the time spent is well
worth while when looking at the finished result, and all the better if care is
taken in contouring the soil surface to enhance the overall effect. Usually
the highest point will be just behind the largest trees, sloping down to
smaller trees at the side and rear and to the edges of the pot.

To complete the picture, the soil should be carefully mossed. It is more
effective to use a darker moss under the trees but it really should not be
necessary to add gravel, stones, little figures or other artifacts to suggest a
scene. The planting should be sufficiently realistic and beautiful in itself. Let
the imagination supply anything else if it will.

Other styles The principles given for group plantings are also applied to multiple trunk, raft and other styles of bonsai, which rely in part for their effect on a number of trunks. A combination of the group planting ideals, with the principles of the training of a formal or informal upright style bonsai will be found to work well.

Raft-style bonsai A raft style bonsai follows the principles of a group planting but is more difficult to execute because the "trees" are branches of a single tree, joined by its trunk, which has grown roots along its length. The choice of tree for this treatment should be carefully considered, the most suitable being one whose branches grow mostly to one side of the trunk and the lowest branch of which is not unduly long.

Initially the selected tree should be laid on its side and studied, and any branches growing underneath that are not required, or small insignificant branches, should be removed. Twiggy growth on the lower one-third of the remaining branches can also be cut away. Any wiring required should be carried out at this stage, care being taken to wire each branch separately.

A deep wooden box should be prepared, long enough to hold the tree on its side, together with its root-ball. The bark on the underside of the trunk can be slit in several places and the cut areas treated with rooting powder to help stimulate root development. The tree should then be positioned in the box so that its trunk is horizontal. Soil, which should be very sandy, is added until the trunk is covered by an inch or two (2.5 to 5 cm) with the branches protruding through it.

The time taken for sufficient roots to develop from the trunk to support the branch growth without the assistance of the original root-ball varies according to kind. Trees such as maples will take one to two years, whereas a Japanese white pine may take from five to 10 years. During the waiting period, considerable training can be given to the branches, from bending to trimming and pruning.

When sufficient roots have formed to support top growth, one end of the box can be removed and the old root-ball cut off. The end of the box is then

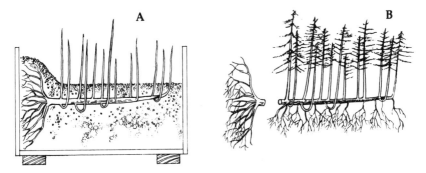

A. *The preparation of a bonsai for training in the raft style.* **B.** *The tree when roots have developed from the trunk and with the old root ball removed. It is now ready for further work to be done on the branches.*

A 100-year-old specimen of Juniperus chinensis *which is trained in the raft style.*

replaced and the newly-created raft can be left in it for a further period to ensure success. Then it can be removed and potted into a shallower training box or a selected display tray. No stressful training should be attempted until the tree has settled in its new container, but branches, if set in position, can be unwired and any necessary trimming carried out regularly.

Planting bonsai over rock In complete contrast to the aforementioned methods of training trees is the technique of planting them over a piece of rock so that the roots appear to clasp the rock before disappearing into the soil below. Most bonsai collectors acquire likely pieces of rock and keep a selection in their garden, so that when one is needed it will be well weathered.

Almost any tree can be used, but a maple, especially *Acer buergeranum*, will produce very fast results. The ideal tree is young and vigorous with plenty of low branches and long roots. Should the latter be lacking, they can be induced by planting in a very deep box or even in the ground for a period of a year or so.

This Pinus thunbergii *bonsai has the appearance of a raft planting but is, in fact, three separate trees planted by the author in 1979.*

The ideal rock is hard and non-crumbling, with an interesting texture, preferably dark in colour and non-symmetrical in shape. While a small rock is easier to handle it should be remembered that although the tree will grow, the rock will not and selection must be made accordingly.

The tree should have the soil washed off its roots and it and the rock should be studied together to decide the paths the roots are to follow. This having been decided, the tree should be put aside, its roots protected from drying out by covering them with moist sphagnum moss or similar material and the rock prepared for the planting.

The roots are to be attached with wires, which must be securely fixed to suitable points on the rocks. For this 4 in (10 cm) lengths of wire can be bent in half and secured to the rock with epoxy resin, leaving the ends free. Alternatively, if the rock has many fissures, a small piece of lead can be wrapped around the middle of each wire and hammered into a fissure using a centre-punch. The lead covering of some wine and spirit bottle corks is eminently suited for this, as it is of an easily worked thickness.

Before positioning the tree on the rock, prepare a mixture of natural clay and peat, with water added until it is very sticky. When this is ready, place the tree on the rock and wire the roots into position. Do not cut off over-long wire ends. It is useful to leave them tucked to one side which makes their removal at a later date much easier.

The entire rock should now be covered to a depth of about ½ in (1 cm) with the prepared mixture of peat and clay and the base of the rock with the ends of the roots hanging down is placed into a container of soil, which covers the root ends. The exposed area of clay is finally covered with sphagnum moss, which must be securely tied in position with twine or string. The tree should be given careful attention for a month to six weeks to ensure it has not been unduly affected by the root disturbance and then it can be treated as a normal bonsai.

After a year or so, depending on the kind of plant being trained, the moss should be removed and the clay and peat mixture washed away in order to check the roots. Any necessary adjustments can be made and the rock re-covered, or, if these are not needed, a display pot can be selected and the tree transplanted. Such plantings are generally more effective if there are a few thick roots rather than many little ones. Over the years insignificant roots can be removed to achieve the best effect.

Another way of using rock is to plant a tree or trees into one with natural hollows and crevises in it, using the rock as a container. The resulting effect may require a combination of the skills used in group plantings, root over rock plantings and upright bonsai training. Of primary importance is the critical selection of the rock and trees with the object of creating a mountainous landscape or something similar, but one problem with this type of planting can be watering. The trees are frequently growing in a very small amount of soil and in hot weather can dry out very quickly. Standing the rock in damp gravel or a shallow pool of water can help overcome this by keeping the rock cool and providing a moist microclimate, but a careful watch should always be kept for possible drought signs.

Growing bonsai in tufa Tufa rock is frequently used for various types of planting. Tufa is a sedimentary limestone which, however, can be used for planting even lime-hating plants such as rhododendrons. It is soft and porous, and, when freshly cut, easily worked with a chisel, screwdriver or similar tool. Its appearance is like that of a sponge, and when weathered it is a most attractive warm grey colour.

Initially, the collector may experiment by growing one tree in tufa, using it instead of a pot. Such bonsai are attractive, their surface roots radiating over the rock before disappearing into it. After many years, the bonsai roots may actually break or split the rock but this, far from being a worry, merely affords an interesing opportunity to present the bonsai in a different manner. Tufa may, however, be used in many far more exciting ways, creating a variety of effects.

For instance, the bonsai enthusiast may care to try creating a mountain scene in tufa. This is a pleasurable activity for spring time and the effect is almost immediately apparent and appreciated. A number of trees are suitable

A bonsai trained in the root-clasping-rock style. It has been established
for many years.

for this type of work. Among the conifers there is a wide range – junipers, yezo spruce, *Picea jezoensis*, and other *Picea* and *Abies* species and varieties. There is a greater freedom of choice than with conventional bonsai plantings and it is acceptable to make use of some of the dwarf conifers for this purpose, possibly in combination with bonsai undergoing training. Alpine plants are also effective and some suggestions of other suitable plants for tufa plantings will be found on p. 109.

Preparing tufa for planting is a simple process. The selected rock should be hosed down to rid it of rock particles stuck in crevices and cavities. It then shows its "grain" to best advantage. The rock should now be placed

A BEECH GROUP

Fagus crenata
(Japanese beech)

This group of trees, the only one owned by the author which was not assembled by her, was imported from Japan in 1978. It is a most interesing example of the different skills that can be used in grouping trees, showing the effective use of quantity, size, shape, colour and texture for the formation of a complete picture.

The trees vary between 20 and 40 years of age. Regular pruning has ensured that there are no unsightly scars to mar the smooth, white trunks, an important point to consider when creating a group that is intended to be at its best in winter. These trunks have a marked colour and texture contrast with the rich brown, sharply-pointed buds. The group is well put together to create a natural woodland effect with smaller trees leaning outwards, and larger, stronger trees reaching upward.

When the group comes into leaf, the pruning has to be carried out with great care. No bud is allowed to develop more than one or two leaves or the twiggy, branching effect would be quickly lost. The leaves, when green, are smaller and finer than those of the common beech, *Fagus sylvatica*, making *F. crenata* very suited to bonsai training. In autumn the foliage turns a beautiful, soft golden-yellow before taking on the usual brown of beech hedgerows. They remain on the group during the winter months before falling in spring as new leaves appear.

The group is deceptive in size, always appearing smaller than it really is. It currently has a maximum height of 27 in (68 cm) and width of 32 in (80 cm) and is potted in a shallow, oval brown kataoka container whose clean smooth curves and quiet colour offer no distractions from the complex beauty of the planting. It is exhibited regularly, usually in autumn or winter, but, as yet, has received no name.

A BEECH GROUP

Fagus crenata
(Japanese beech)

"THE BIG CRAB"

Malus
(crab apple)

"THE BIG CRAB"

Malus
(crab apple)

This interesting bonsai was purchased from a private collection a few years ago. It had been imported from Japan some years previously by the collector, but never exhibited as its beautiful blossoms appeared too early in the year to coincide with any major show.

Expert examination of the fruits suggested that it might be some form of *Malus sylvestris*, but examination of the blossom the following year did not support this theory. It may be a natural hybrid or a little-known Japanese form.

To own such a bonsai and not be able to exhibit it in flower was a frustration too great for the author to put up with, and she planned accordingly. The tree was pruned quite hard as its branches had become rather long and, except when in leaf, gave it an unkempt appearance. It was then for a period pruned minimally, and in due course flower buds were formed in the winter of 1979.

It was kept during the winter of 1979/80 in the coldest spot in the garden. During March it was placed in a refrigerated unit when the flower buds were swelling. Temperature was controlled as the buds developed, ranging from 33 to 38°F (.5 to 3.5°C). The tree was examined every day and removed from refrigeration for watering approximately once a week. No fertiliser was given, it having been heavily fed in the autumn in preparation for what was to come. When the bonsai was finally removed from refrigeration it was watered and placed overnight in a cool room to warm up the soil in the pot. It was then loaded and taken to the Chelsea Flower Show where the flower buds opened exactly as required. Afterwards, it was allowed to remain outside for 18 months before being displayed again, this time with a substantial crop of crab apples, in the autumn of 1981.

The tree is of unknown age and large dimensions. The present height is 36 in (1 m) and it is currently potted in a rectangular unglazed Kataokaware pot of a reddish-brown colour, 21 in (52.5 cm) long by 14½ in (36 cm) wide and 5 in (13 cm) deep. The trunk is 12 in (30 cm) in girth, measured 1 in (2.5 cm) above soil level, so it is perhaps not surprising that this substantial tree is irreverently referred to by its owner as "The Big Crab". When in flower or when carrying its well-coloured and well-proportioned apple-like fruits, it is spectacular.

Pinus parviflora *growing in a piece of tufa rock. The shape of the tree is enhanced by the angular rock.*

the correct way up, and if the base is not flat enough, it may be worked on with a brick, a file or similar rough, hard object. If the rock is too large to lift easily, it should be placed in its permanent position before planting as rolling it over or lifting it on sacks later on could damage new plantings.

Once the rock is in position, the plants to be used should be assembled and studied so that any special features they possess can be displayed to maximum effect. The novice may fall into the trap of doing the obvious, i.e. putting a tall tree at the highest point of the rock and a weeping tree at the side, using natural hollows in the rock for planting without thought as to where they are. If such ideas present themselves, it is better to reconsider and to try holding a tall, slim tree behind the rock near, but not at, the top; or a weeping tree on an uphill slope that then falls away. Such positioning stimulates the viewer's imagination far more, looks more realistic and is generally more satisfactory.

When the first plant positions have been decided upon, holes should be made in the tufa. These are easily carved out with an old chisel or screwdriver with the aid of a lightweight hammer. Holes need not be as large as the pots from which the plants will come, as a considerable amount of soil can be shaken off. Planting involves putting the roots of the tree into the hole with as little damage as possible. Wrapping the roots in a tube of paper facilitates this process and once they are in position the paper can be removed. Dry soil should be added carefully with the help of a slim trowel or chute of paper and eased in between the roots with a chopstick. When the hole is filled up, a little moss can be added to the surface soil, then pressed and held into position with bent wires until established. Should the planting be on a vertical surface, a very sticky mixture of clay, peat and water can be applied before the moss is positioned to prevent soil falling out of the hole. When the whole rock has been planted it should be watered with a fine spray to moisten the soil around the roots of the plants.

Bonsai trees planted in this manner should be trained in the same way as conventionally planted trees. They will, however, require less trimming as growth is slower and shorter-jointed with tufa plantings. If dwarf conifers are used they should look after themselves if correctly selected for their growth habit, but a little bud-nipping occasionally may be an advantage.

To maintain the planting in good health, the rock should be watered in dry weather; and during the growing season occasional weak liquid feeds may be applied, watering the whole rock, not just the planted areas.

Tufa rock plantings have a number of uses. They are ideal presents for plant-minded friends, being original, attractive and easy to maintain, and can also be used as raffle prizes in bonsai clubs as a way of raising funds. A large, well-planted piece can make a rather boring front garden look very interesting, even if only standing on a simple "pool" of gravel within a "sea" of concrete slabs.

Small tufa plantings can be stood in shallow water or on damp gravel. They should never be stood on bare soil as during rainy periods the latter is splashed on to the rock, marring its appearance. Standing on grass is disadvantageous because of the difficulty of cutting it round them.

Dwarf conifers and other plants for planting in tufa Among the dwarf conifers, the following are recommended, making interesting, simple-to-maintain plants chosen for their growth habit and foliage: *Juniperus communis compressa*, the Noah's Ark juniper, a very slow growing plant which has a slim, candle flame shape and fine, needle-type glaucous foliage. *J. recurva coxii* has similar foliage to *J. rigida* but it is of dwarf form and has a weeping habit. For a situation requiring something more bushy, choose *Chamaecyparis obtusa nana gracilis*. To create the same effect, there are some broad-leaved shrubs which will assume tree shapes. The use of daphnes or rhododendrons will enable a rock planting to have different coloured flowers and different seasons of flowering, depending upon which species or cultivars are chosen.

Alpine plants which can be used are many and various and it is not the intention to give an exhaustive list here, but rather to provide some ideas which can be expanded on by use of works of reference. For silver foliage there are plants such as the raoulias, antennarias and the smaller helichrysums. The genus *Saxifraga* deserves special mention here as it is invaluable in rock plantings, whether it be for its silver-encrusted rosettes, its mossy hummocks of white, yellow or pink flowers or the green rosettes of the species, which will act admirably as a foil to other plants. Other kinds which will thrive on tufa include the smaller androsaces and drabas and certain of the very small species of *Dianthus*.

Training mame bonsai Mame bonsai require skilled training and are a challenge to the bonsai grower. The majority are grown from seed or cuttings or wild seedlings, although occasionally a really tiny, old, wild tree may be found and eventually potted as a mame bonsai.

Seeds are normally planted directly into a tiny pot. Cuttings, once rooted, are transplanted, but once growing in the mame pot all trees should be cut back early in the growing season to encourage dwarf growth and branching. For two or three years, side shoots may be removed, after which they may be allowed to grow. Such training will produce a tree with better proportions.

Leaf pruning of deciduous trees should be carried out in summer, inducing a second crop of leaves which are smaller and with better autumn colour. This also discourages summer growth of shoots and is an aid to retaining the diminutive size of the bonsai.

Zelkova serrata and Japanese maple make very good mame bonsai. Zelkovas are normally trained in the broom style. For this, a seedling in its tiny pot should have its shoot tied to a small cane to ensure a straight trunk. The crown of the tree is trained by repeated pinching out of shoots. Leaf removal (leaving the stalk) can be carried out two or three times if the tree is vigorous. This induces dense bushy growth. The branches on such a small tree can be trained by bending with the fingers, wiring not being necessary. Maples are trained in a similar way, the leaves being removed only once in the summer.

The conifer *Cryptomeria japonica*, though a vigorous tree, reaching considerable height in its native Japan, can be readily trained to form an excellent formal upright mame bonsai. A seedling cryptomeria should be induced to branch thickly by removing the leader with all its branches in mid-spring. Many new branches will shoot from the trunk before the end of summer, and the following spring three of the lower ones should be selected for retention. These will become the lower left and right and rear branches of the tree, and their positions determine the ultimate shape of the tree. All other branches and the leader should again be removed and pinching of the new growth on the selected branches should also be carried out to encourage good shape. The following season the remaining branches should be selected for retention, completing the branch structure of the bonsai, and from then on the cryptomeria is trained and developed by pinching out new growth. In this way, a well-coloured and well-shaped mame bonsai can be developed within about five years.

Juniperus species make attractive miniatures, several forms being suitable, and they will provide a pleasing contrast in winter to the bare deciduous trees. As in larger sizes, they can be trained in many styles.

On a very tiny bonsai, flowers or berries can be a surprising and exciting feature. There are a number of trees and shrubs which will flower and fruit from a very young age, among which *Pyracantha angustifolia* and *P. coccinea*. Both root readily from cuttings and bear their tiny white flowers and brilliant fruits readily. These pyracanthas and also cotoneasters are effective when trained in cascade style, which diminishes the rather angular growth habit.

There are several forms of Kurume azalea for training as bonsai. Small-leaved forms can be propagated from cuttings and the resulting plants will flower from two to three years of age. Again, tamarisks are attractive as

A 12-year-old form of Juniperus chinensis cineria. *This specimen is just 6in (15cm) tall.*

weeping bonsai. For mame bonsai the early (May) flowering *Tamarix juniperina* is easier to work with than the later-flowering kinds which, as they flower on the current year's growth, would be rather straggly and untidy at flowering time. This can also happen with *T. juniperina* (though it flowers on old wood) but it is more easily avoided.

One feature of mame bonsai is the possibility of creating an almost instant effect with suitable material, for interesting seedlings can be potted and immediately look attractive. Of course, such trees will improve dramatically with further training, but, as their charm is so immediate, this period of training can be a time of great pleasure for the owner.

The health, care and potting of mame bonsai differs somewhat from the needs of larger bonsai and is dealt with in Chapter 4 (see pp. 62 and 63).

Perennial chrysanthemums Chrysanthemums, when trained as bonsai, differ in one essential aspect from the norm, in that it is important to grow the plant to its final size and shape in the first year. Once a chrysanthemum stem becomes woody it is very difficult to develop it further so for the first year the accent is on producing a shapely specimen. Cuttings are taken in November and rooted in peat and sand in a greenhouse. Once rooted and established, they are, unlike chrysanthemums trained for cascades, pinched out to induce regular branching and a replacement leader. This process should be repeated five to six times during the months of most active growth, which is from spring to September or October. While still green, branches or trunks may be wired to produce curves and other effects, the wiring being carried out very carefully.

In subsequent years the chrysanthemum is trained by regular pinching to encourage more shoots, and it will require feeding regularly to maintain good growth. A bonsai chrysanthemum in good health will retain its old leaves after blooming, an indication of good flowering to come the following year. They are not hardy and should be kept in a frost-free environment during periods when they would be at risk. Basal shoots should be removed whenever they appear, as these will weaken the parent plant.

Annually, in springtime, the "trees" should be repotted, replacing part of the old compost with new. However, after a few years they will lose more and more vigour (indicated by branches failing to produce new shoots) and new plants should be trained to replace them.

Cascade chrysanthemums These are grown and flower in a single year and as they attain considerable size during this time, special attention must be paid to their feeding and potting. After flowering from September through to November, these chrysanthemums produce shoots from the roots. The best ones for producing cascade chrysanthemums are those furthest away from the plant, and these should be cut off without roots and propagated in a mixture of sand and peat or leaf-mould in a greenhouse. If shoots are taken with roots attached, they will tend to produce more growths from their base, which will be detrimental to the ultimate size of the plant.

To obtain the largest plants, cuttings should be rooted singly in 4 in (10 cm) pots. They require shading from hot sun, but otherwise as much light as possible. Once rooted, the plants should be potted into a good loam. John Innes No.2 potting compost would be suitable, and if it seems rather heavy some leaf-mould may be added. After giving the plants two weeks to settle in the pots, liquid chrysanthemum fertiliser should be given, and feeding be continued regularly throughout the growing period.

By spring the growing plants should be hardened off prior to moving outside as soon as the possibility of frost damage is past. At this stage they should be up to 6 in (15 cm) high, with lateral shoots. They require potting on into 7 or 8 in (18 or 20 cm) pots, using a similar loam, and with as little disturbance as possible to the root system. Feeding should be increased to weekly.

Many cascade-trained plants can be seen in this fine exhibit of chrysanthemums staged by the Borough of Slough at one of the Royal Horticultural Society's Westminster shows.

By early May the plant should be large enough (about 10 in [25 cm]) for training to commence. The leader should not be pruned, but lateral branches require pinching at the fourth or fifth leaf.

By the end of May when the plants are 18 in (45 cm) high, support must be given. A thick piece of wire may be inserted into the pot and bent to an angle of 45 degrees about 6 in (15 cm) above compost level, and the plant should be tied to this with stem ties. As the chrysanthemum grows, it will be necessary to enlarge and develop the support to become a framework for the cascade, using bamboo canes which are light and easy to work with.

Pinching must be carried out throughout the summer with the final shape constantly in mind. In Japan it is usual to pinch the upper branches at the second leaf while the lower branches may grow one more leaf. During this period the growing framework supporting the plant must be gradually lowered until it is horizontal, when the plant will again need potting on, this time into a 12 in (30 cm) pot. If a really large specimen is desired, the ultimate pot size would be about 15 in (38 cm). At each re-potting old compost should not be removed and the root-ball should be retained intact. More compost should be added to fill the space in the larger pot.

When flower buds are well formed, the stem may be lowered. The strong wire on the underside of the curve gives support to the stem and must remain in place. Lowering should be carried out in stages to minimise the risk of splitting or breaking, and it is essential that chrysanthemums are protected from wind at this stage. Once lowered, plants should be placed

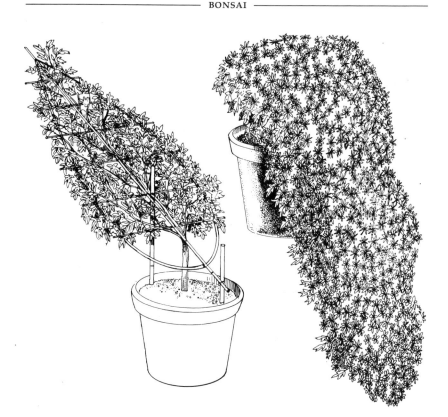

LEFT: *A cascade chrysanthemum at a formative stage. Shown here is the supporting structure made for its branches.* RIGHT: *Cascade chrysanthemums are fully trained and displayed when about one year old.*

facing south until they are flowering, when they can be moved into their display positions.

PRUNING TECHNIQUES

The maintenance of good shape, once achieved, is an important aspect of bonsai care. It is also a comparatively simple and very pleasurable occupation, the technique used depending on the growth habit of the tree. An interesting side-benefit of bonsai ownership is the accumulation of a general knowledge of trees, resulting in a greater appreciation of them when seen in the countryside or in a city park.

Firstly, when we are discussing pruning we must consider those trees whose growth continues throughout the summer months. Mainly of a deciduous nature, these include elm, hornbeam, zelkova, young maples, and mature trident maples and larch. The coniferous Japanese cedar (*Cryptomeria japonica*) is also included here. These trees should have new growth taken back to the chosen level. If shoots are allowed to develop too much and are then removed by pruning, the distance between the leaf joints becomes too great and the desired tapering twiggy structure does not develop, the winter silhouette becoming more like a leafless privet hedge. The process of pinching out new growth (usually with finger and thumb) continues through the summer months, the main growth period, however, being late spring and early summer.

Beech trees have two periods of growth during the year, the main one in spring and a later, less vigorous one in mid-summer. All growth but the first leaf should be pinched from the growing bud as soon as it is possible as a delay will cause removal of the buds which develop very rapidly in the tip growth only.

Some of the conifers, such as *Juniperus, Picea* and *Taxus* follow the same habit of growth, so the pruning is similar for each. When shoots protrude beyond the selected line, they should be pinched out with finger and thumb. This encourages bushy dense areas of foliage, giving the bonsai an appearance of maturity and substance.

Pines are maintained somewhat differently. Vigorously growing pines, such as *Pinus thunbergii* and *P. sylvestris* produce "candles" in spring time. These elongate for a period, after which the needles (the year's growth of foliage under normal circumstances) begin to extend. The candles should be removed by pinching or cutting at the stage before the needles extend. This will have the effect of causing three or four new buds to form around the point of removal, which will develop later in summer into much smaller candles. These should not be removed. Buds will form on top of them and these will become the following year's long candles in spring. They should be removed as described, provided the tree is healthy and growing well.

This process produces dense short-jointed growth but, due to the natural growth habit of pines, it tends always to be in an upward direction. To correct this, the tree should be wired in alternate years after the summer "drop" of two-year-old needles. In Britain this is usually in September. The new growth should be wired so that each branch is persuaded to reach outwards, instead of upwards, rather like the outstretched fingers of a hand. This helps to admit light to the branches, which in turn encourages the formation of new buds from older wood, maintaining and increasing the density of the foliage. By spring the branchlets will be set and the wire must be removed.

The Japanese white pine, *Pinus parviflora*, should not regularly have its candles removed. Instead its maintenance consists largely of wiring bi-annually in the autumn and removing the wire in the spring.

Regrettably, very few people maintain pine bonsai in the correct manner. In consequence, they begin to take on the appearance of a hedgehog on a stem, and if after some years the tree is then correctly wired, it is found that the branches have the appearance of a deciduous tree in winter, the inner growth having died back through lack of light.

The Japanese maple, *Acer palmatum*, is interesting as a bonsai in that, while young, it will develop shoots throughout the summer months, but when mature it has only one period of growth, in spring. Mature Japanese maple bonsai should be treated in the same way as the spring growth of beech trees (see p. 115).

To create a bonsai from a seedling or young tree requires only a vague mental picture of the eventual shape that it should attain, and an adaptation of the trimming already described. The shape can be built up by judicious pinching and trimming until the tree has reached the appropriate size. However, many years of work can be wasted if the young tree selected has faults of growth which are not corrected at the onset of training. Such faults tend to get worse rather than better over a period of time, resulting in a neat, tidy, small-leaved but unbalanced bonsai. The most common failing seen in young trees selected by the beginner for training is the presence of thick, coarse branches near the top of the tree and rather weary, insignificant twiglets near to the base. In nature the lower twiglets would be shed eventually, and the strong upper branches would grow skywards to form the structure of a large tree. In a bonsai, however, the trainer must create in a small tree the appearance of maturity, signified by larger lower branches and a fine twiggy crown. As was said earlier, on a young tree intended for a bonsai, strong upper branches should be removed. This gives the lower branches a chance to develop.

NOTES ON GENERAL APPEARANCE Many bonsai are well shaped and attractive until one looks at the base. An ideal bonsai should have radiating roots from the base of a trunk that tapers upwards, giving it an appearance of strength and maturity. Some, however, are neglected in this respect, and one easily rectifiable fault is when one or two roots emerge from an inch or two (2.5 to 5 cm) above soil level, causing a narrowing of the trunk below

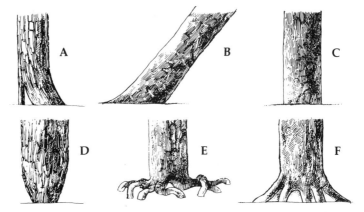

A. *The small root causes the trunk to be narrow at the base.* **B.** *This appears unstable as only one side of the trunk has radiating roots.* **C.** *This has the appearance of a stick placed in the ground.* **D.** *This has an even uglier appearance.* **E.** *Tangled roots.* **F.** *How the trunk should spread into the soil and also have a good root structure.*

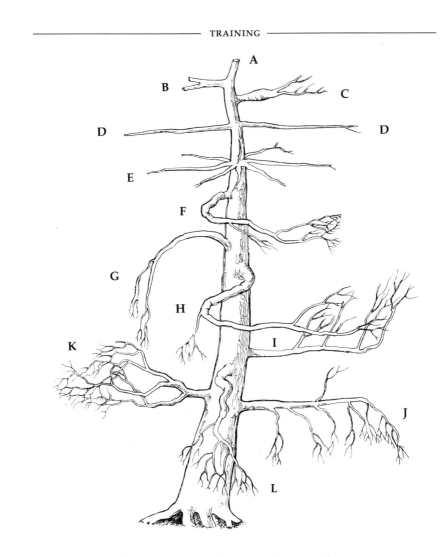

A. *Shinnashi (lacking apex).* **B.** *Shinkire-eda (stubby branch).* **C.** *Gyaku bosori-eda (branch with reversed growth).* **D.** *Kannuki-eda (bar branch).* **E.** *Kuruma-eda (wheel-spoke branch).* **F.** *Miki kiri-eda (branch crossing trunk).* **G.** *Han-en-eda (semi-circular branch).* **H.** *Hiji tsuki-eda (acute-angled branch).* **I.** *Tachi-eda (upward growing branch).* **J.** *Sagari-eda (hanging branch).* **K.** *Karami-eda (tangled growth branch) and* **L.** *Metsuki-eda (eye-poking branch).*

them. Such roots should be removed as soon as the tree has a good enough alternative root system to be able to manage without them.

Some trees, especially those which are container-grown as nursery stock, have roots which are entangled and wound round the base of the trunk. When they have become hardened by exposure to light this fault is impossible to correct, so action should be taken in redirecting them at re-potting time while the tree is still young and its roots thin and pliable.

Should an otherwise nicely shaped bonsai have a trunk with parallel sides like a cylinder, time can effect a cure if the trainer keeps the crown and upper branches of the tree very well pruned, while allowing the lower branches to develop considerably. This will ensure that the lower part of the trunk thickens faster than the upper part, so improving the shape.

Badly positioned or wrongly shaped branches can mar the appearance of an otherwise interesting bonsai. These include eye-poking (metsuki-eda), when the offending limb comes directly towards the viewer from the front of the trunk below eye level, and bar branch (kannuki-eda) the offending branch being positioned exactly opposite to, and level with, another branch. Kuruma-eda is a number of branches radiating from the trunk like the spokes of a wheel, while a trunk-crossing branch (miki kiri-eda) might be acceptable in a tree in the windswept style but not on other bonsai.

Misshapen branches are also undesirable. There are those where the twiggy growth appears tangled (karami-eda), dangling (sagari-eda), or up-growing (tachi-eda) and those whose actual shape is faulty, such as han-en-eda, with a silhouette like a semi-circle; hiji tsuki-eda, an elbow shaped branch; or gyaku bosori-eda, a branch growing outwards and then back towards the trunk. Shinkire-eda, a stubbed branch, may be the fault of the trainer, as may be shinnashi, a tree without an apex. These and other faulty branches should be removed or their shape corrected early in the training of the tree.

The choice of pot is of utmost importance to a bonsai, and one should be selected to enhance the tree. This should not be trained initially in the specially selected container in which it is to be finally planted but allowed to develop first in a simple, plain-coloured, shallow, round pot. The selection of suitable containers is dealt with at length in Chapter 8.

CHAPTER SEVEN

SPECIAL TECHNIQUES

After the bonsai enthusiast has grown and trained a number of small or medium-sized bonsai, he will develop more confidence to tackle ambitious projects. For these there are a number of techniques used in the collecting and training of larger bonsai which are well worth learning as, when skilfully used, the results are dramatic.

TREES FROM THE WILD It is satisfying to obtain a mature bonsai in a short period of time, but while with careful cultivation young trees can be encouraged to achieve a reasonable size within a few years, achieving maturity – to be seen for example in a gnarled bark – is a process requiring time. However, there are two ways of obtaining ready-made mature trees on which to work and the first of these is to collect from the wild specimens dwarfed by circumstance. Little equipment is needed, but it cannot be too often stressed that the necessary permission must be obtained once a suitable tree is located, if you wish to dig one up.

Traditionally the season for collecting bonsai from the wild is early spring, shortly before the tree has started into active growth, but in Britain there is some cause to doubt whether this is always the optimum time. There has been a trend in recent years for English springs to be cold, wet, sunless and long. Established bonsai have not enjoyed these conditions so it is not unreasonable to suppose that transplanted trees will not thrive on such unpleasant weather either.

Experiments carried out for the last five years with bonsai transplanted during June or July have shown encouraging results. During June of 1976 (the hot summer) 150 trees, some very large, were lifted from very dry ground and found to have such long tap roots that these could not be extracted. The roots were sawn off just below soil level, the branches were pruned and the trees, both deciduous and coniferous, potted and placed in full sun. The amount of fibrous root per tree was negligible but, sprayed every half hour with water, many were pot bound within six weeks. The experiment was 96 per cent successful and further such experiments in successive years showed that the installation of mist propagating equipment was justified for this use.

The use of mist propagating equipment also ensures success with softwood cuttings of those plants which it had formerly been found difficult to root. This equipment works on the principle of maintaining high humidity around the cutting (to keep it alive until it has rooted) and cooling the foliage with intermittent mist. In combination with a bench temperature of around 65°F (18.5°C)and plenty of light many cuttings root readily given this treatment.

Bonsai collectors may care to experiment with the digging up of large wild trees during the summer months. Automatic misting equipment is, as has been said, very helpful, but if this is not available and provided someone is standing by to spray a transplanted tree very regularly, there is little reason why a collector should not be successful.

Tools and other materials required for digging up a tree consist of a spade, trowel and handfork (all of which should be clean and sharp), strong secateurs and a small saw for pruning branches and/or roots. You will also need a selection of polythene bags of different sizes, a ball of string, some wet sphagnum moss and a bottle of water. Should the terrain be rocky, it is useful to include a club-hammer, cold-chisel and a small crowbar with which to move or split rock.

When digging up an old tree, it is advisable to prune away any branches that will definitely not be required in later training. The collector should take care to do as little damage as possible to the tree's roots, for the greater the root-ball the better the chances of success. Many wild trees have few fibrous roots and rely for their meagre existence on three or four long roots which may travel a long way from the trunk. Should this be the case, it is sensible to follow the course of such roots and extract as great a length as possible. These can be wrapped around such root-ball as may be present.

Once digging is complete and the tree lifted, the root-ball should be wrapped in wet sphagnum moss and placed in a polythene bag. This should be firmly tied in several directions to prevent unnecessary movement and root damage within the root-ball. Should the tree still have foliage, or the journey home be a long one, it is helpful to spray the upper part of the tree with water and enclose this within another bag. Black polythene bin liners are ideally suited for this purpose.

Once home, the tree should be unwrapped and any obviously damaged roots trimmed at an angle with the cut side uppermost. It should then be potted, using a container large enough to take the root-ball but not so large that the roots will not grow to fill it in a fairly short space of time. The soil used for potting will depend on the tree. With coniferous trees, for instance, a mixture consisting mainly of leaf-mould and sharp sand is preferable to a loamy mixture.

Normal procedures for newly potted trees should now be followed, watering thoroughly but carefully to ensure that the root-ball and the newly added compost are completely saturated. After this the tree should be stood outside in a sheltered shady area to recover. This is helped by the regular spraying of the branches and foliage, but the soil in the pot should only be watered when it is becoming dry.

AIR-LAYERING Another method of obtaining a fair-sized, mature-looking bonsai quickly is by the process known as air-layering. This is successful with many types of tree and, as has already been mentioned, is particularly of use in obtaining good wisteria bonsai. The best time of year for air-layering is June or July. The equipment required is simple to obtain, and consists of clear and black polythene sheeting, moist sphagnum moss, hormone rooting powder, tape, string, or other binding material, a sharp knife and a pair of scissors.

Having selected a branch which seems ideally suited to training as a bonsai, make two parallel shallow cuts around the branch, just underneath a leaf node if posible. The bark between the two cuts can be removed. The width of bark strip removed varies with the thickness of the branch but on a branch of 2 in (5 cm) diameter a strip ½ to 1 in (1 cm to 2.5 cm) wide should be taken away.

Clear polythene sheeting should be firmly fixed to the branch below the stripped area and rooting powder applied to the latter before it dries out. Moist sphagnum moss can now be wrapped round it, which is easier to remove later if finely chopped before application. The clear polythene sheeting is now drawn up over the whole thing and fastened firmly around the branch above the cut to hold the moss in place. Finally, a sleeve of black polythene should be secured over this to exclude light. It can be removed from time to time for examination of the mossy area for signs of developing roots without causing any disturbance. When plenty of roots have formed the branch can be cut off below the air-layer and potted up. Easily-removed sphagnum moss can be taken away prior to potting.

AIR/ROOT GRAFTING Air-layering techniques can also be applied in another way, in conjunction wth grafting. Straightforward grafting of scion and stock is not frequently used in bonsai cultivation, but on occasions root grafting is practised. For the enthusiast who wishes to try any of the following procedures, a period of practice with more conventional grafting is almost essential to gain the necessary expertise to achieve reasonable success.

Maidenhair trees (*Ginkgo biloba*), like some other kinds, do not respond

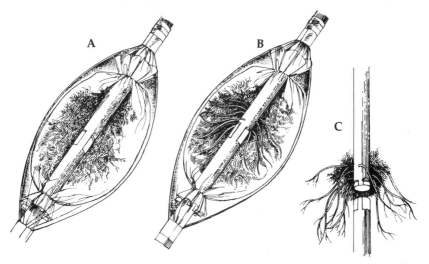

A. *A branch prepared for air layering.* **B.** *The roots beginning to appear above the ringed area.* **C.** *The rooted branch ready for potting.*

"WIRGA'S ELM"

Zelkova serrata

This lovely example of a broom-style *Zelkova serrata* was imported in 1976 by a bonsai nursery and exhibited for a year before being sold to a private collector. The author purchased the entire collection in 1979 when the owners moved abroad.

Zelkova serrata is often trained in this style and the tree shows the straight tapering trunk, the flaring out of branches from a single point and the fine, twiggy branches that are the hallmark of a good broom-style bonsai. At soil level the radiating roots can also be seen, gripping the ground and demonstrating the maturity of the tree.

Potting of such bonsai is of considerable importance if their clean lines and elegant light appearance are to be correctly enhanced. The container used for this tree is a shallow, oval, straight-sided, incurved tray 18 in (45 cm) long by 13 in (32.5 cm) wide and 1¾ in (4.5 cm) deep, hand glazed on the outside in a subtle shade of dull pale blue.

This tree is beautiful to look at at any time of year, but holds especial charm in autumn, when its leaves take on the yellows and rich russets characteristic of *Z. serrata* before leaf-drop comes, which leaves it perhaps even more lovely in winter. The shape can then be seen at its best, the fineness of the twigs contrasting sharply with the slim, straight trunk.

Probably about 50 years of age, the outline is steadily improving. In 1979 the top of the tree was somewhat flattened and the width was greater. Training is being continued with the aim of raising the top by another 1 or 2 in (2.5 or 5 cm). It grows far more than this in a year but if long shoots are left on the tree, they will appear straight and over-strong, giving too great a contrast to the fine delicate branching which is at present a feature of this tree.

It has been named "Wirga's Elm" in recognition of the private collector who at one time owned it, and who cared for it meticulously during that period. It stands 22½ in (56.5 cm) high, and should remain in its present container for many years.

"WIRGA'S ELM"

Zelkova serrata

"HORACE"

Juniperus rigida
(needle juniper)

"HORACE"

Juniperus rigida
(needle juniper)

This old tree in the moyogi style with driftwood effect, was imported by the author from Japan in 1971 as the first large, old Japanese bonsai in her collection. Such trees have to be selected from photographs and, as this is sometimes a hazardous procedure, its arrival was awaited with nervous anticipation.

It was sent from Japan in an extremely fine, dark brown hand-made taikoda pot, 12 in (30 cm) in diameter and 4 in (10 cm) deep, signed by Mr Kataoka of the Yamaki pottery, in which it remained (though re-potted every two or three years) until 1978. By then a slightly larger pot was required and a rectangular un-glazed uchien style one, made by the same pottery, was selected. It is 16 in by 12 in by 4 in (40 by 30 by 10 cm) and has a greenish tinge to its grey-brown colour

At the time of import the bonsai was 24 in (60 cm) in height, with a wide, straggly crown shaped like a saucer and lower branches which were rather short. The lowest (left-hand) branch was, in fact, considerably less than half the width of the crown, but over the next few years the crown and branches were considerably changed. Always a vigorous grower, it responded well to a programme of training designed to improve the crown by controlling its width, thus changing the unfortunate, saucer-shaped silhouette to the present more balanced shape.

The lower branches grew and lengthened, eventually correcting the upside-down look when the span of these became greater than the diameter of the crown.

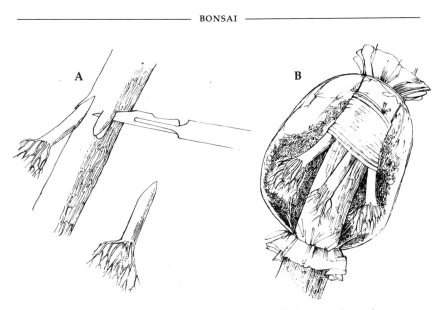

A. *Roots prepared and grafted into a branch. These will be covered in sphagnum moss.* **B.** *The grafted area, enclosed in sphagnum moss, bound and covered.*

readily to air-layering. It is, however, possible to "root" a branch of a big ginkgo tree by the process known as air/root grafting. For this, it is necessary to obtain a number of healthy growing roots, each about half the thickness of a cigarette and each having a good fibrous root system. The fibrous roots are wrapped as for the air-layering, leaving 2 or 3 in (5 or 8 cm) at the cut ends of the main roots protruding from the bundles in each case. Next, an appropriate branch of the ginkgo tree is prepared by cutting into the branch in an upward direction, a tongue of bark being lifted slightly, leaving it attached at its upper end. The root is prepared by cutting slices from the upper and lower side of the end protruding from the polythene, forming a flattened "point" to insert under the flap of bark. This operation should be repeated several times until a number of roots have been inserted around the circumference of the branch. All must then be firmly secured by binding with raffia or grafting tape.

The whole assembly of grafts and bundles of root-ball should now be wrapped in clear polythene, tied above the grafted area and below the root-balls. Support must be given to the root-balls whose weight might otherwise dislodge them from the point of the graft. The clear polythene should again be covered with black polythene, which may be removed as before for inspection. Air/root-grafting can also be used to shorten the trunk of an over-tall bonsai, using some of its own roots grafted to a selected point on the trunk.

BRANCH GRAFTING Branch grafting is used more than is perhaps realised in correcting a wrongly shaped bonsai or even in the creation of a new one. Should a tree be obtained with a fine trunk but few or no branches, this can be cultivated until a number of young, long healthy shoots have grown.

These, being flexible, can be bent until a part is in contact with the trunk at a point where a branch is needed. A matching piece of bark is carefully removed from both shoot and trunk and the two cut surfaces bound tightly together until they have united. The shoot is then severed from the tree at its original point of issue as it has become a new branch in another location. This is called "air inarching" and is applicable to many varieties of tree, but perhaps is most frequently used in the production of ginkgo and ornamental acer bonsai. In the latter case a well-shaped and sizeable trunk of *Acer buergeranum* can become a specimen of *A. buergeranum variegatum* by the process of inarching long shoots of the latter variety (which in nature grow very slowly) on to the trunk of the former. It should be remembered that such trees however cleverly they may be contrived, will from time to time produce shoots of the stock plant, which must be removed. Skilfully executed grafts will be difficult to locate, even on close examination.

THE TECHNIQUE OF JINNING Collectors frequently admire fine old specimens of juniper or pine with areas of dead wood contrasting with the healthy green of the foliage. Some of the dead wood on these trees will be the result of natural die-back but some is the result of skilful bark-stripping by the bonsai craftsman. This process is known as jinning, and its use is normally confined to coniferous trees, especially junipers.

A jin is a dead tip of a branch or sometimes a whole branch, and is not difficult to produce. The branch should be broken and the end pulled off. The bark is then stripped off with a jinning tool, which is a pair of pliers with rounded ends. Slivers of wood are then peeled off strip by strip until the jin is of the required thickness and girth. While still moist, the jin can be wired and bent into shape. The wire should be carefully applied to avoid damaging the soft wood.

Jins can be preserved by an application of lime sulphur in midsummer, which should be put on with a brush on a hot, sunny day. The surface of the soil in the pot should be covered to prevent the chemical dropping on to it.

Another use of a jin is to reduce the height of a tree, giving a struck-by-lightning effect, but it must be mentioned that, in creating jins, there is a strong case for "least used, best served". The novice jin creator can get carried away with his new skill and the results are usually artificial-looking and out of keeping with the tree.

TWO OTHER AGEING TECHNIQUES There are at least two other techniques commonly used to give an aged appearance. The first is the process of stripping off a considerable amount of the bark. The area is then whitened as with a jin, and is known as sabamiki. The technique may be used on its own or in conjunction with jin. Novices trying sabamiki effects are sometimes over-enthusiastic and continue removing the wood from the trunk after stripping the bark. Taken to extremes, this causes it to look a little like an upended dugout canoe and is rarely successful.

Wild trees may have certain features of great charm and beauty marred by a single, straight, over-heavy branch arising from the trunk. Removal of this branch may leave an unsightly scar, and jinning may not be appropriate. Under these circumstances another special technique known as uro can be used. The offending branch is removed close to the trunk and a hole carved deeply into the latter where the scar would have been. This hole must be cut in such a way that any rain running into the hollow can run out again, and the shape of the perimeter is of great importance. When the wound is healed by bark growing over the edges, the effect should be natural and in keeping with the character and shape of the bonsai. As with jin and sabamiki, uro, when used with sympathetic care, can produce very good effects, but when unimaginatively undertaken can look very artificial.

All three of the techniques just outlined, once carried out on a bonsai, are rather difficult to change. Jinned branches could of course be cut off, and it would be possible to fill a hole with some inert substance to allow bark to grow over it, but if these solutions have to be resorted to, it would have been better not to have carried out the procedure in the first place and to have spent longer considering the possibilities open to one in developing a particular bonsai.

INDUCED TRUNK SPLITTING Bonsai, trunks of which have split with age, have much appeal. This effect, too, can be induced by the skilled bonsai trainer and is not infrequently practised on pines and junipers. There is a specially-designed tool for the job, known as a trunk cracker, which looks rather like a pair of electrician's cutters. This is an expensive and, in Britain, a rarely seen tool, but chisels can also be used. With these, the tree is prepared by lying it on its side on a work-bench. A block of wood of suitable thickness should be arranged underneath the area of trunk to be split and padded vices used to hold the tree firmly in position. A chisel is then positioned and, using a hammer, gently tapped until it has passed through the trunk. It can be left in position while two more chisels are applied, one on each side, and then the first chisel can be removed and a small wedge inserted. The process is continued until a split of the desired length has been made. Jinning one side of the trunk will cause the wood on that side to die, while the other, continuing to grow, will over the years cause the split to enlarge and become an interesing feature of the bonsai.

LEAF PRUNING One feature of a well-displayed deciduous bonsai in summer is the wealth of small clear-coloured leaves. These are produced by cutting off (in June or early July) every leaf on the tree, which must be in good health to tolerate the treatment. Not even small or undersized leaves should be left as the bonsai would channel its resources into producing shoots at these points rather than in forcing dormant leaf buds to grow. A bonsai on which leaf pruning is to be practised may with benefit be given a weak dose of fertiliser four or five weeks before the operation, but it must not be fed too soon before or after pruning. Having removed all the leaves, extra care must be taken when watering for a week or two. The need for water will be reduced and there is a danger that overdoing it could cause rotting of the roots.

The new crop of leaves will be smaller and better-coloured than the first and their autumn tints will also be of a richer hue.

Many people are aware that bonsai, when partially trained, may with advantage be planted in the open ground for one, two or more years. The primary benefit is in the more rapid thickening of the trunk. There are disadvantages, however, if proper care is not taken while growth is progressing.

In Chapter 6 mention was made of the improvement which can be made to the taper of a trunk if the crown of a tree is kept well-pruned while the lower branches are allowed to spread more vigorously. Once a tree is established in the ground, apical growth becomes very vigorous and that of lower branches less so. It is, therefore, of importance to maintain pruning of the crown to retain and improve taper and also to keep the important relationship between the greater diameter of the lower branches and the lesser girth of the upper ones.

It is good practice when trees are in the open ground to move them annually to prevent too great a loss of fibrous roots. To ignore this is to allow the development of tap roots, making a bonsai more difficult to re-establish in its container.

Better results will be obtained if, before planting, the roots are prepared in the following way. On removing the bonsai from its pot, tease out the root-ball as much as possible with the object of locating five or six good roots which radiate from the base of the trunk in a reasonably uniform manner. Remove flush with the trunk any that emerge from above those selected (see the reference to faulty trunks, p. 116) and root prune the rest of the root-ball, except for the selected roots, as hard as is considered safe. When planting, it is advisable to encourage the selected roots to go deep, so it is necessary to dig a deep hole. Refill the middle of the hole, allowing the long roots to hang down like the tentacles of a jellyfish round a central mound of soil. The rest of the hole can then be filled in in the usual way.

The tree should be left undisturbed for two or three years, by which time the selected roots will have become sizeable tap roots. These radiating from the base of the trunk, will enhance the appearance of the bonsai, as strong spreading roots give the impression of stability, strength and age. They can, though, be pruned just below the surface of the soil without disturbing the other roots and the tree be left for one more season during which fibrous roots will develop from the cut ends, enabling it to be easily re-established in a bonsai pot. Should the tree be a maple or zelkova it can be cut out of the ground, only going 1 in (2.5 cm) below the surface of the soil and while in full leaf, then being potted into a propagating mixture of peat and sharp grit. It should be placed in a sunny greenhouse with automatic mist propagation and a new fibrous root system will develop within a few weeks. Larch trees appear to be sensitive to misting equipment and if this method is used it is advisable to place them so that mist does not fall on the foliage. They will, however, benefit from the humidity in the air.

AN EXPERIMENT WITH BEECH Bonsai enthusiasts who have greenhouses may be interested in a recent experiment in the use of mist equipment with transplanted beech trees, which had an unexpected result. Beech (*Fagus*

A specimen of Zelkova serrata, *now 3ft 6in (1.15m) tall, though dug up as a 7ft (2.25m) high tree in 1976. It was very severely pruned and re-potted before the photograph was taken in September, 1981. If certain precautions are taken, trees can be lifted successfully and re-established in early summer.*

sylvatica) of various sizes and ages had to be cleared in midsummer at short notice from an area of ground in which they had grown undisturbed for four years. Tap roots had developed which were substantially removed and top growth was reduced by half. Potted and placed under intermittent mist the already-wilting leaves revived within a few hours. Within a week leaf buds appeared in profusion on both the trunk and branches of every tree. These duly opened, producing one or three leaves per bud, and after three weeks the dormant buds for the following spring growth were apparent at the tips of the new shoots. The beech trees, originally pleasantly shaped but sparsely branched, now offer a profusion of short-jointed, twiggy growth, considerably improving the potential of the trees as bonsai. To date the procedure outlined above has not given similar results with other species.

THE QUEST FOR KNOWLEDGE As we know, for centuries, the techniques of growing and training bonsai have been developed and improved by the Japanese masters. The British have acquired some of these skills but they are by nature a conservative race, feeling their way cautiously in order to understand fully an alien approach. They are also, however, a nation of inventors and innovators, a great advantage with an interest such as bonsai, where results depend so much on the ingenuity and taste of the trainer.

With the current upsurge of scientific progress in horticulture, the bonsai enthusiast is offered an unique opportunity of developing totally new methods of growing and training trees as bonsai, formerly inconceivable to the most skilled master. As X-ray tracers and the electron microscope help scientists to understand the innermost working of the living plant, so this knowledge is passed to others practised in the art of interpreting it and applying it to the better growing of crops and the maximising of yields. Some of this technical know-how may well in time be of use in bonsai work and though in Britain at least bonsai training does not have the commercial significance of corn or potatoes, like art, literature or music it must continue to expand and develop, allying a constructive and innovative approach with the consolidation of ideas of proven worth.

CHAPTER EIGHT

PRESENTATION

Presentation is an important aspect of bonsai cultivation and could be considered to cover three different points. The first and most important of these points is the appearance of an individual bonsai in relation to its pot and the manner in which it is potted to display and enhance the tree. In Britain this very important aspect of cultivation is frequently overlooked. The reason for this is not immediately apparent but could conceivably be due to the long gardening traditions of our islands. Collectors may feel that the cultivation of bonsai trees is a simple and undemanding form of horticulture which is interesting and pleasant to carry out, without realising that the use of every horticultural skill is, to a bonsai specialist, the equivalent of using paint, brushes and canvas to the artist. These are the tools of his profession, but, although using these tools in an activity enjoyable for its own sake, the finished product should be a work of art, capable of being appreciated by those who know nothing of cultivation as well as by those who do. Like a painting, a bonsai should be displayed in the manner most likely to accentuate its lines and underline its character.

Once a bonsai tree has been sufficiently trained to acquire that indefinable quality known as "presence", thought must be given to the choice of pot most suited to it. The majority of trees will be potted in rectangular or oval pots and choosing between these would seem a simple task. But differences in depth, width, design and colour, even in these two basic shapes, widen the number of possibilities, and until the collector has potted a number of trees into display containers and developed an instinct for the most suitable pot, some comments and guidelines may be helpful.

In most cases the size of the pot is indicated by the dimensions of the tree. There are bonsai with unusual dimensions or features, an extremely thick trunk in relation to height for instance, or an attractive yet unusual bend or other focal point. For most bonsai, however, it will be found that the length of the pot should be a little over two-thirds the height of the tree, measured from the base of the trunk to the top of the crown, vertically. If the tree should happen to have widely-spread branches but be lacking in height, the length of the pot should be a little over two-thirds of the width of the branch span. It should never be the same as the height or width of the tree.

With the exception of multiple-trunk trees (including raft, group plantings and so on) the depth of the pot should match the diameter of the trunk. With young but shapely bonsai a slightly deeper pot can with advantage be used, as the tree will be vigorous and its trunk thicken more quickly. Pine

An old bonsai (Juniperus chinensis) *with areas of dead wood in the trunk enhancing the effect of maturity. It is being retrained after being mistakenly grown as a dwarf conifer in a garden for many years.*

trees can also be grown in pots slightly deeper than this formula would suggest. Visually, this gives them a more rugged or solid appearance.

The width of a pot is determined by the potter, but the majority of rectangular or oval pots conform to a ratio of three to two, i.e. a pot 12 in (30 cm) long will be 8 in (20 cm) wide. There are some variations on this and where there is an opportunity for choice, the width of the pot should be narrower than the greatest (horizontally drawn) distance between the tips of forward and backward sloping branches.

The shape and style of pot should relate to the style and character of the bonsai. A tree with an interesting curve in its trunk will be enhanced in an oval pot, perhaps also with curved sides. A pine, as mentioned previously, will take a slightly deeper container, and is usually best in a rectangular pot without a lip and with straight sides. The corners and feet of the pot should be uncluttered and simple and the final effect one of ruggedness and power.

Broom-style elms are almost always potted in very shallow and preferably straight-sided and lipless oval trays, the soil sloping gently up to the base of the trunk, giving a tranquil effect to a beautifully shaped bonsai whose appeal lies, not in its curves or massive branches, but more in its delicate elegance and perfection.

Cascade-trained trees are potted in deep pots to give visual balance between the pot and long trailing branches. The branches should hang below the pot base and their tips should not touch the stand. Such pots may be round, hexagonal or square. Round pots emphasise the gentle curves in a formal cascade while square pots give an impression of ruggedness.

With raft, twin-trunk and other styles involving a few trunks, a long shallow pot is the ideal, usually about one-third of the height of the tallest trunk in length. A very long shallow pot may, however, be preferable to create a "field alongside trees" effect.

Literati trees are invariably potted in very small, shallow, round or square pots. An interesting feature of these bonsai is that if one ignores for a moment the long thin winding trunk and concentrates on the crown of the tree, this, if it could be detached, would look well potted in the same pot and some guidance in choice can be taken from this.

The choice of shape and size of containers is, as already explained, of great importance to the finished effect, but it is also necessary to consider other features of pots once the basic dimensions have been established in relation to a particular bonsai.

The most obvious feature is colour. The vast majority of pots seen in Britain are Kobeware, which is an unglazed dark brown, and they are available in a wide selection of shapes and styles. There are also a number of rectangular, dull apple-green and dark blue pots which, though far more limited in their range of style, may be useful to have on certain occasions.

There is a general agreement amongst bonsai specialists and collectors, both in the East and in Britain, that coniferous bonsai are best suited to plain pots of subdued and natural colours. This, for collectors in Britain, generally means using Kobeware dark brown pots, although a few collectors are now making use of the very elegant and high quality Yamaki pots which are of more subtle colouring. These range in colour from sandy brown to gunmetal grey and silvery grey and add much to the appearance of a good bonsai. Kataokaware is also of interest for its colour range in natural shades, not quite as subtle as the Yamaki pots, but still of good quality and considerable interest. It is in the use of coloured (glazed) pots that disagreement arises. This is perhaps because of the limited range of glazed pots available in Britain and in general their rather ordinary quality.

The finest glazed pots are, in fact, antique Chinese ones. These are scarce and extremely expensive, as also are antique Chinese unglazed pots, but if ever they are to be found at a realistic price they should be purchased. They are works of art in their own right and those over 200 years old are known as Kowatari by the Japanese. Less aged Chinese pots are grouped into Chuwatari and Shinwatari, the latter being made in the first quarter of the 20th century by the Chinese, specially for the Japanese market.

Glazed pots are of particular use for the potting of flowering plants. Bonsai with white flowers will harmonise with light yellow or willow-green glazed containers, while plants such as winter jasmine (*Jasminum nudiflorum*) or forsythia would be enhanced by a dark green glaze. Red flowers are attrac-

A multiple-trunk Acer buergeranum *bonsai displayed to good advantage with its root spread well featured. The soil surface is neatly gravelled and the oval tray oiled.*

tively set off against a light or dark blue glaze. Some trees grown for foliage effects, such as maple or ginkgo, can also be shown off to advantage in willow-green or dark blue pots, but those bearing brightly-coloured fruits are enhanced if an earthenware type of container is chosen.

There is considerable reluctance on the part of British collectors to maintain a collection of pots so that, at repotting time, a suitable choice is at hand. A growing but regrettable attitude is the tendency for them to feel that they have achieved something by spending as little money on bonsai pots as possible. This does not entirely relate to economics, though naturally this must be taken into consideration, but would appear to reflect a lack of awareness of the difference a really well-chosen pot can make to a bonsai. There is perhaps also a feeling with a number of collectors that their bonsai will never be good enough to do justice to good pots. This lack of confidence is understandable but far from being true. There are many attractive bonsai in small private collections that certainly merit a quality container.

Various small features of a bonsai pot can reflect the character of a bonsai. For instance, some containers have, instead of rectangular feet which give a visual appearance of strength and power, more ornate sloping feet almost Chinese in character, known as a "cloud feet". These exude an air of elegance

An unglazed Chinese chuwatari 19th century pot, flanked on either side by glazed antique Japanese square containers.

and will enhance a tree already showing that quality.

A number of rectangular pots show variation in the shape of their corners. There are those with rounded corners which soften the rugged impact of the container (known as uchien if the top is incurved or nadekaku if it is straight sided) and those which, although the corners are more conventional, have a lip with the corners cut off, visually shortening the length and depth of the container (sumiire).

A very striking container is the taikodo, a round pot best described as looking like a tyre. It may have curved sides (like a trolley tyre) or have straight sides and incurved top, like a car tyre. This dramatic type of pot is very effectively used for sloping-trunk bonsai and, in very small sizes, for literati bonsai.

Pots with incurved lips (fukuroshiki-bachi) are often avoided because of difficulties with repotting. Bonsai need to be cut out of such containers when pot-bound, but as this is not a difficult procedure these pots should not be excluded from consideration. Their very neat finish can be flattering to the right bonsai and, perhaps unexpectedly, they have special advantage for those bonsai which are frequently exhibited. The trees once established in their pots, cannot fall out if they are accidentally tipped over.

For group planting and similar multi-trunk styles of bonsai, large and very shallow containers referred to as "trays" are generally used. These may be rectangular or more commonly oval, and as with bonsai pots, the sides range from having outward or inward curving lips, may be completely straight and undecorated, curved outwards and upwards or curved outwards then inwards. Careful selection will enhance a group, curves generally flattering those plantings where curves in branches and trunks are also a feature, straight sides or lips flattering more formally trained bonsai.

The trainer of bonsai should purchase attractive containers wherever possible and store them for future use. It may seem strange, but if a particularly good pot is obtained merely because it appeals to the collector, it is rarely very long before a bonsai is found which is totally suited to that container.

Whether this is because such a pot has made an impact on the collector's mind and he can, without realising it, visualise what he would put in it, or whether this is just chance, one cannot know, but it is curious the frequency with which this happens.

Having selected a suitable pot for his bonsai, the collector must endeavour to pot the tree in the most flattering way. This phase involves not only the positioning of the bonsai in the right way but the manner in which the contours of the soil are made and the skilful use of moss. A really well-trained tree rarely needs the addition of rocks, stones or pebbles to give quality. These are usually either applied because the owner likes the stone and desires a place to put it where he can see it, or because the tree is deficient in some important aspect, and a stone or rock will distract attention from the fault.

When a collector has potted his better-trained bonsai into suitable containers, his attention should now turn to the manner in which these are presented in his garden. In the most ideal circumstances, those bonsai which are only partially developed or perhaps in training pots should be separated from those which have been developed further and are in presentation containers. Where bonsai are to be displayed on a patio, benching may be erected near the centre or to one side of it. A little thought given to the matter of construction materials of such a bench to blend with the surroundings can produce something simple, inexpensive and worthwhile. The owner of a rustic patio may use sawn-off tree trunks to support wooden staging, a period residence would be enhanced if the bonsai were to be displayed on carved stone slabs resting on stone plinths, and those collectors living in modern houses, where use has been made of artificial paving, may well find that the use of trays filled with appropriately coloured gravel and elevated on matching paving or a few bricks will give just the right effect. Where a lawn is an important feature of a garden, its cool appearance can be heightened by the use of rock along one side. The top of a low wall of natural rock, with low and high points along its length, is a most attractive place to display bonsai. Bonsai in training may be placed on tiered shelving or staging, where all round light is available, and the trees can be easily reached.

Some collectors may wish to give that part of their garden adjacent to the bonsai collection an aura of the East, and stone, gravel and sand can be used to reproduce in a small way the appearance of a Zen garden. One important point to remember, however, when attempting this type of layout, is that Zen gardens, unlike Western ones, which are designed to draw the viewer into and through them and have unexpected visual delights in unexpected corners, are intended to be viewed only from a single point, and their purpose is purely contemplatory. Bonsai are also intended to be viewed in this way, and, ideally, the tree should be so positioned that an imaginary point half-way up the front of the trunk is at eye level. This fact, though acknowledged in the West, is rarely practised.

This is probably due to the British tradition of decorating their room with large vases of flowers, rather than single blooms, which has been interpreted, in bonsai terms, as enjoying a massed display of them rather than the appreciation of the qualities of a single bonsai. In the East, in the skills of bonsai, Ikebana (flower arranging) and landscape gardening, as well as in other arts such as calligraphy, equal importance is given to the effect of space around an object and to the shape and quality of that space as there is to the object itself. In Britain, in bonsai circles at least, this important aspect of display is largely ignored.

STAGING EXHIBITS AT SHOWS The enthusiast may wish to enter his trees for competition. But, although his bonsai may conform to regulations as to size, age or kind laid down by the organisers, the exhibitor should not consider entering anything that is not healthy, not correctly potted, nor displayed to its best advantage.

When suitable bonsai have been selected, he (or she) should attend to details. Pots should be wiped clean and, if of unglazed Kobeware, they may be oiled. A clean cloth dipped in vegetable oil and wiped over the surface will give a fine gleam to the surface, and if initially this creates too great a shine, after two or three days as the oil soaks into the porous container, the optimum effect is created. Moss on the soil should be short and moist and look well established. Dead, damaged or oversized leaves on deciduous trees should be removed, as should brown needles on pine trees.

A bonsai can be enhanced when displayed on a suitable stand. Cascade-style trees do, of course, need these, but other more conventionally-shaped bonsai may be placed with advantage on a thick polished "slice" of tree trunk, a low wooden stand or even on a woven bamboo or linen mat. The same is true when a bonsai is brought indoors for display for an evening or two, and the effect can be further improved by placing a small, complementary object near to the pot. This may be a tiny pot of dwarf bamboo, an antique oriental bronze or an attractive stone. Whatever the object it should be carefully placed to enhance the bonsai and should not become the focus of attention. Being small, it accentuates the size of the bonsai and at the same time forms a harmonious picture with it.

As was mentioned earlier, the use of model houses, boats and people to add "realism" to a bonsai, while affording amusement to children not yet old enough to appreciate the beauty of the trained tree, is unnecessary and a distraction. A group planting, for example, should be so convincing on its own that a spectator can almost see a path running through it. Another viewer of the same group may in his imagination see a fox slinking past a tree, and a bonsai that can give to its audience such vivid pictures as these needs no further visual embellishment. It has totally convinced those who look at it that it is a forest and not a number of little trees in a pot.

Perhaps the greatest challenge that the collector may have to face is the designing, equipping and staging of a large exhibit comprising many bonsai, possibly the property of both himself and other club members, at an agricultural show. This type of display relies not only on the quality and presentation of the trees exhibited, but on many other factors as well. Because of the size such an exhibit is likely to be I shall give some guidance to those who may have to undertake such a task.

Initially, it is wise to go to other shows and to study exhibits staged by clubs or professionals. The would-be exhibitor should try to work out why a certain stand is good (or bad) and endeavour to understand just why such an impact is made with a particular bonsai or arrangement of bonsai. This will help him to plan the exhibit he wishes to create himself, bearing in mind any limitations imposed upon him by the numbers, types or quality of what he has to show.

Major agricultural/horticultural and town shows held in England and Wales are often good places to set out bonsai exhibits of quality staged by professionals, clubs or societies, or both.

To exhibit bonsai effectively requires space, and the most commonly used size of stand would be 30 ft (9 m) long by 6 ft (2 m) wide. Such stands are usually positioned against the sides of the exhibition building or marquee and, are known as wall sites or side stands. Bonsai cannot.be viewed properly when on the ground, so tabling is needed. Tiering of some sort is helpful, as are plinths and boxes. The aim should be to allow as many bonsai as possible to be clearly seen by the onlookers.

To ensure a complementary-coloured background it will be necessary to provide a piece of material a little over 30 ft (9 m) long and at least 4 ft (1.25 m) wide. Should the display be in a marquee, this should be fire-resistant. Another piece of material, usually black, is needed to cover the table legs. This should be 42 ft (12.5 m) long and 3 ft (1 m) wide (most tabling is 2 ft 6 in (75 cm) high, the extra few inches allowing for fixing). More covering is needed for the tables themselves (30 ft [9 m] by 6 ft [2 m]) and the tiering (top, front and sides). Should the exhibitor decide to spread gravel on his tables (perhaps to create a more "natural" effect) he will need to transport this to and from the show, and once there it must be spread on some form of covering, such as old cloth or polythene sheeting. If he decides to use gravel, one hundredweight of a fine grade will, with care, cover about 75 sq. ft (7 m^2). If "peagrit" is used (little pebbles about the size of a pea) one hundredweight (50.802 kg) will only cover about 50 sq. ft (4.65 m^2). The more unevenly laid the bottom protective covering is, the more gravel will be needed to cover the lumps and creases.

A 30 ft (9 m) by 6 ft (2 m) stand will require about 50 bonsai to fill it. These are likely to range from big bonsai to mame bonsai, with the majority of the trees being 12 to 21 in (30 to 52.5 cm) in height. If, as in the case of a club exhibiting for the first time, the majority of bonsai available are small, a 20 ft (6 m) space should be requested and a similar or slightly lesser number of bonsai will be required.

Of special interest to the onlookers will be the range of plants exhibited. A balance should be created between evergreen and deciduous trees, and within each category there should be as much variation as possible. Trees in flower or fruit are desirable, as are trees with attractively coloured leaves (such as maples) or variegated foliage. And several different bonsai styles should be represented, including group and rock plantings and cascade trees, as well as various informal upright trees. The pots used should also feature a range of styles and sizes.

Labelling should, to be strictly correct, give Latin names only. According to the most recent ruling by the Royal Horticultural Society on the matter, the ages of the trees may also be stated on the labels. However, there are

"THE BLACKBIRD PYRACANTHA"

Pyracantha angustifolia
(firethorn)

The sight of a well-shaped pyracantha bonsai in full flower is a never to be forgotten sight. The tiny white flowers cover it, yet because of their size do not overwhelm it. Instead they show up the shiny, bright green young foliage to best effect.

This particular pyracantha was purchased in 1974 from a bonsai nursery because of the shape of its trunk. At that time the lower branch was far less developed than at present and the left-hand branch did not exist. The whole plant had a somewhat unbalanced appearance and was potted in a dark, royal blue, glazed, round, pudding-basin-like container, which did not display it as effectively as it might.

The bonsai was trained and developed slowly, and enjoyed a number of different containers before finally being potted in the dark green-brown Yamaki container seen in the photograph. This is a high-class, rectangular container with cloud feet and a simple out-turned lip that gives the tree an elegance unusual in one with so twisted a trunk.

Perhaps surprisingly, it is named "The Blackbird Pyracantha" as a result of reading a newspaper article on the subject of blackbirds preferring bonsai pyracantha berries to the more usual garden sort. The article was written as a direct result of the tree being displayed at the Chelsea Flower Show of 1978 when it carried a large crop of bright red berries, saved in this case from the blackbirds by netting. It is an example of a bonsai which, though not being of great appeal in the first instance, had the essential good points to enable a thoughtful and reasonably skilful owner to develop it until it became attractive and interesting. The chief virtue at the time of purchase was the long, gently tapering trunk. Some good surface roots were present and others developed, especially on the left-hand side, where initially there were none.

Flowering bonsai should be pruned with some care to ensure a good display each year. This one always tends to flower best in alternate years, and advantage is taken of this in the years when there is less blossom to prune the tree with its future shape and development in mind. It currently stands 24 in (60 cm) high and its pot measures 15½ in by 9½ in by 2½ in (39 cm by 24 cm by 6.5 cm).

"THE BLACKBIRD PYRACANTHA"

Pyracantha angustifolia
(firethorn)

"THE SOMERSET BEECH"

Fagus sylvatica
(common beech)

"THE SOMERSET BEECH"

Fagus sylvatica
(common beech)

This interesting bonsai is about 15 years of age and is currently about 36 in (1 m) tall. It was collected by the author in November, 1977 from a hedgerow which was due for clearance. Growing under an avenue of mature beech trees at about 700 feet (210 m), it had fortuitously taken root in leaf-mould covering some large boulders. This prevented the growth of a taproot, the tree instead developing a spreading base and fibrous root system. Its location caused considerable development of the lower part of the tree and a lack of the usual strong upper growth associated with a wild beech.

When found it was larger both in height and in branch span than at present, being approximately 5 ft (1.5 m) high and 4 ft 6 in (1.4 m) wide. On lifting, it was immediately potted into a square pot measuring 10 in x 10 in x 3½ in (25 x 25 x 9 cm) into a mixture of 50 per cent beech leaf-mould, 30 per cent sand and 20 per cent loam. At the same time the overall dimensions were reduced by about 6 in (15 cm).

By April, 1978 the beech was established and twiggy growth was pruned harder and the left-hand lower branches wired to improve their position. Also the tree had a large branch removed from near its crown, reducing the height by another 12 in (30 cm). The following spring (1979) it was re-potted into a rectangular container of 18 in x 12 in x 3½ in (45 x 30 x 9 cm). New twiggy growth was beginning to develop from both trunk and branches, and the bonsai was reduced to nearly its present size, being 3 ft 4 in (1.1 m) high and 3 ft (1 m) wide.

The current pot is of mid-brown, unglazed kataokaware, oval, with outwardly sloping sides and lip and cloud feet, its overall dimensions being 21 in x 16 in x 3 in (52.5 cm x 40 cm x 8 cm).

The bonsai developed well and was first exhibited in 1979 at a late October R. H. S. show while in autumn colour. It regularly holds its leaves, once dead, right through the winter, retaining them until new growth in May forces them to drop. The leaves have a natural tendency to be small and have further reduced since it was originally collected.

In 1980 the height was brought down to its present 3 ft (1 m). In October of that year, when the photograph was taken, the tree was showing the brilliance of its autumn colours and also showing the direction in which further training should lie. It is planned to reduce the height and width still further over the next two or three years. It is named "The Somerset Beech" after the county in which it was found.

disadvantages in this, especially for a club trying to recruit new members. Naturally, the bonsai displayed are the best, rather than the youngest in members' collections, and many of the trees may be of unknown age, having been collected in the wild. When potential members read the label of, say, an eight-year-old elm which happens to be 7 in (18 cm) high, their first thought is usually "if it takes that long to grow a few inches, it's too slow for me." If, on the other hand, the ages are not marked, interested viewers will ask. This gives the collector a chance to explain that the little tree and the big one behind it are in fact both perhaps eight years of age. He planned to grow a big one and a little one and this is the result. Such an answer is almost certain to elicit further questions and may create a real interest in the questioner in the skills of bonsai training.

If the show is of two days' duration, the bonsai will need watering. A spray gun with a "long arm" will do, but a watering-can is more thorough. Before watering the trees, move the labels unless the wording on them is run-proof and the labels themselves incapable of collapsing into a dampened mass.

At the end of the show, all has to be cleared up and removed. Trees, gravel and other material need to be packed into one or several vehicles quickly and safely. If the show has been held in a marquee and the weather has been fine, be prepared for rain during the clearing away period and take a pair of Wellington boots. A thermos or two of coffee is useful at this time, for clearing a stand is hard physical work.

Trees may be transported safely in club members' cars, estate cars being particularly suitable. Should a club have the chance of using a van, a 22 cwt (1117 kg) one will, with very careful packing, transport the entire exhibit and accessories on a 30 ft (9 m) by 6 ft (2 m) stand. But there is unlikely to be room for passengers!

On returning home after a show, bonsai should be returned to their usual positions in the garden and watered from overhead unless it is raining hard. This is to clean the trees, which will be dusty after their stay under canvas or indoors. Occasionally, jolting or knocking while moving them about may have loosened a bonsai in its pot, and any lost soil should be replaced. Keep such bonsai in a sheltered spot until re-established.

One or two shows in a year cause few problems for a healthy tree (an unhealthy one should not be subjected to such stress) but bonsai which are exhibited frequently may respond unfavourably to such treatment. If they are showing signs of distress they should be kept in good conditions in the garden until fully recovered.

Exhibiting bonsai is, by and large, an enjoyable experience. It is always interesting, although it can on occasion be a very hot or a rather wet and muddy experience. It is great fun when a bonsai wins a prize, especially if there are other nice trees in the class, but it is really of little importance if the judges favour another. The collector has still achieved the satisfaction of training a tree, during which time he has derived very considerable pleasure from his hobby.

CHAPTER NINE

PESTS AND DISEASES

Bonsai, when properly cared for, live a long time and, from the point of view of pests and disease infestations, are generally trouble-free. There are, however, a few problems that may arise from time to time, and they are not always tolerant of conventional treatment. The commoner insect, animal and disease problems are given below, along with suggestions for combating them.

INSECT AND OTHER PESTS

Ants The presence of ants on a bonsai is normally an indication that some other insect is present. This is generally an infestation of greenfly or other aphids, which must be removed before dealing with the ants or they will return. Ants do not damage the bonsai by sucking sap or cutting foliage, but they may cause trouble in pots by forming a nest in the root-ball.

Freeing the bonsai of both greenfly and ants is a simple task. Merely submerge the tree, in its pot, in a bowl of water into which has been mixed a desertspoon of washing-up liquid and one of Jeyes Fluid per 3 gal. (13.5l) of water, so that the water completely covers the tree and pot. The tree should remain submerged for half to one hour, depending on size. All ants will leave the root-ball and drown.

Aphids Also known as greenfly or blackfly, aphids can be a problem in spring and early summer, when there is a profusion of soft, sappy, young growth for them to feed on. In bonsai, the varieties generally affected are maples. Bad infestations can seriously weaken these but sprays used on ornamental shrubs or vegetables should not be used as they are for some reason intolerant of them, even if used with great care. The red-leaved *Acer palmatum* 'Chisio' and *A. p.* 'Seigen' are especially sensitive. However, the safest treatment is also a simple one. Fill a bucket with water, to which has been added a desertspoon of washing-up liquid, and hold the tree upside down in the water, swirling it around for a few minutes to dislodge the aphids. The tree can then be rinsed in a fresh bucket of clean water to ensure that no detergent drips on to the potting soil.

Birds By and large, birds are to be encouraged as they eat many pests that could cause trouble. However, on occasions their presence is less helpful.

At nesting time, the moss in bonsai pots seems irresistible to them, and in midsummer they also pull out the moss in search of insects. To protect them, cover the top of the pots with plastic mesh netting, cut to make a hole for the trunk.

Blackbirds are much attracted to the white plastic labels commonly used in seed trays and frequently pick them out. One solution for this problem is to use aluminium labels and bend them over the side of the seed tray or pot. Blackbirds are also fond of pyracantha berries, which they will eat off a bonsai rather than from a neighbouring shrub, so these should be protected by netting in late summer when berries begin to ripen. Members of the tit family are enthusiastic eaters of greenfly, ants and other pests, but vary their diet with the succulent centres of crab apple blossoms, both prior to and during flowering. So these and other blossoming trees such as plum, apple, pear, apricot and cherry should also be protected with netting before and during flowering.

Caterpillars These generally cause little trouble to bonsai, as a lone caterpillar eating a leaf is easily spotted and removed. Some choose to pupate among bonsai foliage, sealing leaves together and lying inside, safe from birds. Crab apples, cotoneaster, pyracantha, juniper and pine seem more favoured for this attention than other kinds, and the leaves when noticed can be pulled apart and the offending pupa removed. Occasionally caterpillars can devastate willow trees, appearing without warning in large numbers and rapidly eating every green part of the foliage. A "cure" can be effected by using the washing-up liquid in water treatment, and the willow will fortunately grow more leaves.

Cats These are a mixed blessing. A resident neutered cat can be advantageous to the bonsai collector as cats are territorial animals and the resident will keep other cats from the garden. It will also learn, with some reluctance, to keep away from newly planted seed trays and may catch mice, which can damage bonsai trees seriously. Strange cats can be a nuisance to seed trays and tom cats can kill a tree through persistent attention to a chosen trunk. Contrary to popular belief, cats do not sharpen their claws on bonsai trees. If visiting cats are causing trouble, a hosepipe effects a remarkable though temporary respite.

Dogs Dogs are usually only a problem if bonsai are kept at ground level. If they are, as they should be, on shelving or tabling of some sort, then dogs are no problem. In fact they may be useful in warning off light-fingered intruders.

Earwigs These may sometimes feed on foliage at night and are attracted to an area by the presence of dead leaves, weeds and other debris in which they nest. Good attention to general garden hygiene should avoid any problems.

Gall Wasps The larvae of these tiny insects live in plant tissues and are the cause of "oak apples" on oak trees. These do not harm a healthy tree, but on a small bonsai they should be removed by pruning the relevant twig.

Hares The hare population expanded enormously after the virtual extermination of rabbits with myxomatosis, and during a hard winter hares will eat tree bark to survive. Trees can be netted or otherwise protected in areas where this is a hazard.

Leaf Cutter Bees These bees live in tunnels in decaying wood, soil or old brickwork and the females cut semi-circular pieces of leaf from certain deciduous trees. These pieces are used to line the nest tunnels. The bees are not gregarious, so a patient half-hour with a fly-swatter may effect a cure. Otherwise try to locate and destroy the nest.

Mealy Bugs These thrive on some indoor plants, including bonsai, and are best removed by hand if seen. They look like pale-coloured small woodlice while immature, and live in small colonies which are covered with a substance looking like white cotton-wool. If left unchecked they multiply rapidly, feeding on sap and excreting honeydew, which encourages the growth of sooty moulds on foliage and stems.

Mice These rodents will, like hares, feed on bark in winter. They chew right into the bark and will go round a trunk or branch, ring-barking it and killing it. To get rid of these pests, use conventional methods such as mouse-traps, poison or a cat. (Many London mice are immune to poison and therefore alternative methods are recommended if you live in this area.)

Red Spider Mite This is a serious plant pest, attacking indoor and outdoor plants, including bonsai, especially when conditions are dry. The mites can be detected from the minute webs they form and they cause the plant to look dehydrated. They will cause serious trouble to junipers and other conifers and should be treated as soon as seen. Evergreen outdoor bonsai are tolerant of spraying with liquid systemic insecticides to get rid of them, but prevention is better than cure and, as we have already seen, the maintenance of a humid atmosphere around the plants during the summer months will help greatly in avoiding this problem.

Root Aphids Some aphids inhabit the soil, eating roots and damaging plants. Indications that they are present are if the foliage turns yellow and wilts. So far as bonsai are concerned a cure is difficult as so many kinds are sensitive to chemicals, but the washing-up liquid treatment may effect good results. The bonsai may then be repotted, using fresh, sterilised soil.

Scale Insects These insects can infest almost any tree and their presence is indicated by a poorly-growing tree and limpet-like scales on the trunk, branches and the undersides of leaves. It is under these that the female scale insects live, and they should be removed using a cotton wool bud dipped in methylated spirits or a lighted cigarette end. The pot should be covered during this procedure to ensure that scales do not drop on to the soil, for the young scales hatch under the mother scale and then undergo a mobile stage, at which time they are known as crawlers. Scale insects also attack indoor plants, some members of the genera *Ficus* and *Citrus* being particularly vulnerable. An infestation of scale insects if left untouched can weaken a bonsai enough to kill it.

Slugs Slugs may eat bonsai foliage and will also cause damage to roots. They are attracted to slug bait so it is best to avoid these pellets (see under June in Chapter 4). Toads eat slugs and many other insects. The installation of a small pool surrounded by a few stones, ferns and grasses will encourage toads to breed there and they may possibly stay around the garden. Frogs are also useful. Spawn of both may be obtainable in spring from local school children. Slugs do not like moving across sharp fine gravel so standing pots on this material makes bonsai less accessible to them.

Snails These are less of a nuisance than slugs but it should be remembered that they do bury themselves in soil. Remove whenever seen.

Whitefly These are related to aphids although the adults resemble tiny moths. They occasionally affect young beech tree and crab apple growth, feeding on sap and secreting honeydew, which is a sign of their presence. Beech and crab apple trees can be sprayed with pyrethrum. Other trees may be cleared with water and washing-up liquid.

Woolly Aphids On bonsai these are seen primarily on pines and crab apple trees, producing conspicuous tufts that look like white wool. Systemic insecticide can be used on both kinds, or these aphids can be removed by hand with cotton wool buds and methylated spirits.

Woodlice These grey, hard-coated, many-legged pests live in damp places and feed on decaying debris. They can cause serious damage to roots and stems of plants, and should be dealt with in the same way as ants. It should be mentioned that bonsai pots should never be stood directly on soil, or there will be constant attacks by both these pests. Bonsai are best standing on gravel, platforms of stone or shelves of treated wood.

DISEASES

Bonsai trees seem to suffer from remarkably few diseases, perhaps due to the generally good conditions in which they are kept. However, a few diseases may appear on weakened trees and these are listed below.

Azalea Gall This is an airborne fungus disease which attacks azaleas, the spores entering plant tissues. After several months galls replace leaves or flowers. They are red or green initially, turning white. Once white, these galls are ready to spread more spores, so cut them off before this occurs.

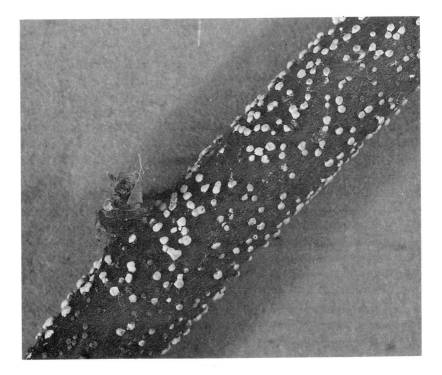

Coral spot, a fungus living on dead wood, which may become parasitic.

Coral Spot This is a fungus, normally living on dead wood, but it may become parasitic on entering living shoots. Bonsai are not normally troubled in this way as dead branches and twigs are removed, but if coral spot appears on a neglected dead branch, that branch must be removed immediately. A careful watch should be kept for the tell-tale raised orange/red spots on living wood, and, if seen, further pruning must be immediately effected.

Crown Gall This is a bacterial root disease resulting in stunted, poor-looking plants. The bacteria enter root wounds and multiply in the gall. A cluster or chain of galls may be seen on the roots. The trouble is aggravated by waterlogging, but is not common in bonsai though it has been seen on the roots of imported cotoneaster, pyracantha and *Juniperus chinensis* trees.

Damping-off This trouble is caused by a parasitic fungus which causes seedlings to collapse. However, they are only likely to be affected if they are planted too closely together or are grown in wet conditions or in high temperatures. Attacks may largely be avoided by watering seed trays with Cheshunt Compound.

Dutch Elm Disease (*Ceratocystis ulmi*) Elm bark beetles – originating from eggs laid in diseased elms – spread this devastating fungus disease by

Crown gall, a bacterial root disease which enters plant tissue through wounds and forms galls (see p. 149).

Azalea gall, an airborne fungus disease of these decorative shrubs (see p. 148).

transmitting the spores as they feed on the young shoots of healthy trees.

The spores gain entry through wounds made by the beetles and subsequently a resin is produced which causes die-back of the branches and the eventual death of the tree.

Prevention rather than attempted cure is appropriate: spray the trunk and branches of the tree with a systemic insecticide during spring.

Mildew This name covers a number of different types of mildew, all of which are fungal diseases identifiable by a dusty, powdery coating on the leaves. It is more prevalent in wet summers and may attack oak, hawthorn, crab apple (and apple) and hornbeam bonsai. All these trees can be sprayed with a systemic fungicide suitable for ornamental shrubs, and badly infected shoots can be cut off.

Tar Spot This is a fungal disease specific to acers. In bonsai, the best control is removing infected leaves with their black spots, and in autumn removing and burning all the foliage of the affected tree. A very dilute copper fungicide solution can be applied in spring as the leaves open, but this could adversely affect a weak tree.

CHAPTER TEN

GLOSSARY OF PLANTS

NOTE: **Composts recommended in this glossary refer to those detailed in chapter 4, p. 54 and 56, the March section of the Monthly Cultural Guide.**

Acer buergeranum (Japanese trident maple) Hardy, deciduous. Very well suited to cultivation in various upright styles and much used for root-clasping rock bonsai. It has small leaves, a fine twiggy habit and features spring and autumn colour.

Propagation	Seeds, cuttings, air-layering
CULTURAL NEEDS	
Re-potting	Once every two to three years in spring before bud-burst, using a standard compost mixture.
Pruning	Small branches during summer months, large branches in winter.
Wiring	Any time.
Fertiliser	Apply May to September.
Pests	Greenfly in spring and early summer.

Acer buergeranum variegatum (Variegated trident maple) Hardy, deciduous. A rarely seen, less vigorous form of the above, suited to upright styles of training. It has small green and white leaves and interesting autumn colour.

Propagation	Grafting
CULTURAL NEEDS	As for *Acer buergeranum*.

Acer campestre (field maple) Hardy, deciduous. Not quite as suited to bonsai training as *A. palmatum* or *A. buergeranum*, yet it still makes a attractive, medium-sized, informal, upright tree.

Propagation	Seeds.
CULTURAL NEEDS	As for *A. buergeranum*.

Acer palmatum (Japanese mountain maple) Hardy, deciduous. Very well suited to bonsai cultivation in many styles. Renowned for its autumn colour.

Propagation	Seeds, cuttings, air-layering.
CULTURAL NEEDS	
Re-potting	Every one to two years in spring before leaf burst, using the standard compost mixture.
Pruning	Small branches in summer, large branches in winter.
Wiring	Any time.

| Fertiliser | Apply April to October. |
| Pests | Greenfly in spring; occasionally scale insect. |

Acer palmatum 'Chisio' (Chisio maple). Nearly hardy. Deciduous. A beautiful variant of the above suited for cultivation in upright style. Renowned for red-coloured foliage in spring.

Propagation	Grafting.
CULTURAL NEEDS	As for *Acer palmatum.*
NOTE	Should be given winter protection

Acer pseudoplatanus (sycamore) Hardy, deciduous. This common tree is easy to grow, and with care will make an attractive informal upright bonsai.

Propagation	Seeds.
CULTURAL NEEDS	
Re-potting	Every one or two years, using the standard compost mixture.
Pruning	Bud-prune in spring. Remove leaves in late June. Branch-prune in summer.
Wiring	In summer; wire-marks easily.
Fertiliser	Apply sparingly in spring and autumn.
Pests	Relatively trouble-free.

Aesculus hippocastanum (horse chestnut) Hardy, deciduous. Easy to grow in informal upright styles. Rather large leaves will dwarf successfully.

Propagation	Seeds.
CULTURAL NEEDS	
Re-potting	Every one to two years in spring before leaf-burst, using the standard potting mixture.
Pruning	Remove apical buds in December. Branch-prune in summer as necessary. Leaf-prune in July.
Wiring	Any time.
Fertiliser	Apply from May to September.
Pests	Generally trouble-free.

Aesculus indica (Indian horse chestnut). Hardy, deciduous. Easy to grow in informal upright styles; leaves are smoother and better coloured than above.

| Propagation | Seeds. |
| CULTURAL NEEDS | As for *Aesculus hippocastanum.* |

Amelanchier asiatica Hardy, deciduous, flowering. Grown for its autumn colour. An interesting and less well-known bonsai.

Propagation	Seeds.
CULTURAL NEEDS	
Re-potting	Spring.
Pruning	Branch-trim in summer, providing the tree is well fed.
Wiring	Summer.
Fertiliser	Keep well fed.
Pests	Relatively trouble-free.
NOTE	Protect from very hot sun. Keep well watered.

Azaleas evergreen, oriental. These are trained as bonsai in Japan, and small-flowered forms can be very pleasing in full bloom.

Propagation   Cuttings.

CULTURAL NEEDS

Re-potting   Annually in late March, using one part each of lime-free loam, peat, leaf-mould and sharp sand.

Pruning   Immediately after flowering.

Wiring   In summer.

Fertiliser   Apply in spring and autumn with a fertiliser high in phosphate.

Pests and Diseases Generally free of pests but may be affected by azalea gall.

Betula pendula (silver birch) Hardy, deciduous. Easy to grow in all styles. Bark becomes silvery in colour and roughens over a period of time. Appreciates a little shade in mid-summer.

Propagation   Seeds.

CULTURAL NEEDS

Re-potting   Every two years in spring before leaf-burst, using the standard compost mixture.

Pruning   Prune young shoots back to three buds; leaf-prune in July.

Fertiliser   Apply from May to September.

Pests   Generally trouble-free.

Betula nana (dwarf birch) Hardy, deciduous. Easily trained small shrub with small, rounded leaves and fine, twiggy growth habit, well-suited for mame bonsai training.

Propagation   Cuttings.

CULTURAL NEEDS As for *Betula pendula*.

Buxus sempervirens (box) Hardy, evergreen. Tiny-leaved tree suited to cultivation as mame or other small bonsai; has small green flowers with yellow anthers in April.

Propagation   Cuttings.

CULTURAL NEEDS

Re-potting   Every two years, using the standard compost mixture.

Pruning   Pinch back young growth in May and late July.

Wiring   Do not wire.

Fertilisers   Apply from April to September.

Pests   Generally trouble-free.

Camellia japonica (common camellia) Hardy, evergreen, flowering. The inclusion of camellias in a bonsai collection offers colour at a time of year when there is little. Rarely well-shaped by nature, they can nevertheless be trained to become interesting and pleasing.

Propagation   Cuttings

CULTURAL NEEDS

Re-potting   Immediately after flowering in a mixture of lime-free loam, leaf-mould, peat and sand. Avoid pruning large roots.

Pruning	Summer.
Wiring	With protected wire in May or June. Remove wire as soon as possible.
Fertiliser	Apply regularly in small doses.
Pests	Scale insects.
NOTE	Lime-hater which dislikes being short of water. Protect from frost in winter; otherwise keep in a cool area out of strong sunlight.

Carpinus betulus (common hornbeam) Hardy, deciduous. Forms a fine-leaved bonsai in all styles. Has flowers followed by pendulous clusters of winged seeds. Very attractive grey bark.

Propagation	Seeds (often slow to germinate).
CULTURAL NEEDS	
Re-potting	Every other year in March, using the standard compost mixture.
Pruning	Prune young growth during late spring and summer.
Wiring	During summer as needed. Bark easily wire-marked.
Fertiliser	Apply in April and September. Avoid excessive feeding.
Pests and Diseases	Occasionally troubled by aphids. Occasionally affected by mildew.

Carpinus laxiflora (Japanese hornbeam) Hardy, deciduous. Details as for a common hornbeam, but more attractive, due to its fine autumn colouring and more silvery-coloured bark.

Cedrus libani (cedar of Lebanon) Hardy conifer. Easily trained to form a spreading bonsai in upright style.

Propagation	Seeds.
CULTURAL NEEDS	
Re-potting	Every second year in March or September, using the coniferous compost mixture.
Pruning	Prune new season's shoots whilst still green. Branch-prune in September.
Wiring	October.
Fertiliser	Apply in April, May and September.
Pests	Relatively trouble-free.

Celtis sinensis (Chinese nettle) Hardy, deciduous. Grown for its fine autumn colour and delicate, twiggy growth, this makes a fine bonsai.

Propagation	Seeds
CULTURAL NEEDS	
Re-potting	Every two years in spring, autumn or, if necessary, in summer at time of pruning.
Pruning	Summer
Wiring	Summer.
Fertiliser	Apply in spring and autumn in small quantities, but frequently.

Pests	Relatively trouble-free.
NOTE	Protect from freezing or hot afternoon summer sun.

Cercidiphyllum japonicum (Katsura tree) Hardy, deciduous. Easily grown round-leaved tree suited to upright styles, valued for the red colour of its foliage in spring and fine autumn tints.

Propagation	Seeds or cuttings.
CULTURAL NEEDS	
Re-potting	Every one or two years in spring before bud-burst in standard mixture.
Pruning	Keep trimmed in spring and summer, leaf-prune in July.
Wiring	In summer, as required.
Fertiliser	Apply in April to September.
Pests	Generally trouble-free.

Cercis siliquastrum (Judas tree) Hardy, deciduous. Easily grown and trained into informal upright styles. Has attractive rounded, rather glaucous, green leaves and will flower in May.

Propagation	Seeds.
CULTURAL NEEDS	
Re-potting	Every two years before bud-burst in standard mixture.
Pruning	Spring and summer. Leaf-prune July.
Wiring	Any time.
Fertiliser	Apply from May to September.
Pests	Scale insect.

Chaenomeles japonica (Japanese quince) Hardy, deciduous, flowering. This and other members of the quince family are popular bonsai as the bright red or pink flowers are long-lasting.

Propagation	Cuttings or suckers.
CULTURAL NEEDS	
Re-potting	Yearly in spring or autumn.
Pruning	Remove long growth, retain short flowering branches.
Wiring	Do not wire.
Fertiliser	Apply phosphate-based fertiliser in late summer.
Pests	Aphids, occasionally.

Chamaecyparis obtusa (Hinoki cypress) Hardy evergreen conifer. An attractive slow-growing tree with finely-marked foliage, suited to all styles. Very rarely seen as trained bonsai in Britain.

Propagation	Seeds or cuttings.
CULTURAL NEEDS	
Re-potting	Every three years in March, using the coniferous compost mixture.
Pruning	Trim twigs with too many leaves; pinch out growing shoots.
Wiring	Wire branches in late March.
Fertiliser	Apply in April and autumn.

Pests   May be attacked by red spider mite in hot, dry spells.

Cistus salvifolius (rock rose) Half-hardy evergreen. Flowering. Makes an attractive informal bonsai with sage-like foliage, and white flowers in May if given sunny but sheltered position.

Propagation   Seeds or cuttings.

CULTURAL NEEDS

Re-potting   Every two years in late spring, with care.

Pruning   Nip new shoots. Maintain in good shape; dislikes hard pruning.

Wiring   Do not wire.

Fertiliser   Apply in April and autumn.

Pests   Generally trouble-free.

NOTE   Winter protection from frost.

Citrus Tender evergreen.

C. limonia (lemon), *C. aurantium* (Seville orange), *C. nobilis* var. *deliciosa* (mandarin and tangerine oranges), *C. paradisi* (grapefruit) and *C. sinensis* (sweet orange).

Propagation   Seeds at 65°F. (18.5°C).

CULTURAL NEEDS

Re-potting   Once every two years in April or May, using the standard compost mixture.

Pruning   During summer months. Leaf-prune in July.

Wiring   During summer.

Fertiliser   Apply in April, May, September.

Pests   Vulnerable to scale insect, mealy bug and red spider.

Cotoneaster horizontalis Hardy, deciduous. Flowering. Very popular and readily-trained in most styles. It has tiny bright green foliage, turning brilliant red in late autumn. Small pink flowers in May are followed by berries which ripen to bright scarlet in August.

Propagation   Seeds, cuttings.

CULTURAL NEEDS

Re-potting   Every two years during March using the standard compost mixture.

Pruning   Trim all young growth as necessary. Branch-pruning in late winter or summer.

Wiring   Wire young growth before it becomes woody. Check frequently as branches wire-mark easily.

Fertiliser   Apply lightly in April and September.

Pests and Diseases Relatively pest-free but the bacterial disease crown gall sometimes seen on imported plants.

Cotoneaster simonsii Hardy, semi-evergreen. Flowering. One of many cotoneasters suitable as bonsai. It has small, dark green leaves and clusters of white flowers are produced in June, followed by orange-red berries. Propagation and cultural needs as for *Cotoneaster horizontalis*.

"THE STATELY MAPLE"

Acer buergeranum
(Japanese trident maple)

This young, formal, upright-styled tree was grown from a cutting taken in 1965 by the author, along with others, from another bonsai. The rooted cuttings were potted and trained, five being retained, not because of their quality but rather because, to her then less-experienced eye, the trees did not reveal their future potential. After two or three years training in pots, they were planted in open ground and were left, totally unpruned, for four years. During that period they became attractive shrubs, some 5 ft (1.5 m) in height.

The trees were then dug up, their tap roots severely pruned and, as it was summery weather at the time, almost all top growth and the majority of lateral branches were removed. New branches formed on the upper part of the trees, and by good fortune in one case these appeared in positions which indicated straight away the direction which the training of the tree should take. Accordingly, these indications were followed and the branches were pruned and pinched to create much-divided twiggy growth. Some wiring was done to bring the branches horizontal.

After four years of this training the maple was beginning to display a little of its future beauty. The spreading roots, after their period in open ground, had developed to a far greater extent than the age of the tree would indicate and were beginning to look mature and strong. It was potted from its training container into a mid-brown kataokaware rectangular pot with a rectangular foot, the severity of line being broken by a discreet Greek pattern. The container measured 16½ in (41 cm) by 3¾ in (9.5 cm) by 29 in (72.5 cm) and the tree was a little below its present height of 28 in (70 cm).

When exhibited, onlookers remarked on the maturity and charm of this particular bonsai. "The Stately Maple" as it is now known, was given its name by Gwyneth Melville-Clark, the owner of a very fine collection of English and Japanese bonsai and widow of the founder of the Bonsai Kai of the Japan Society of London, Mr. Ian Melville-Clark. Over many years she has given encouragement, advice and guidance to many bonsai enthusiasts and on seeing the young tree for the first time she remarked with thoughtfulness and feeling, "What a stately maple."

"THE STATELY MAPLE"

Acer buergeranum
(Japanese trident maple)

THE UNNAMED GINKGO

Ginkgo biloba
(maidenhair tree)

THE UNNAMED GINKGO

Ginkgo biloba
(maidenhair tree)

This old, very thick-trunked bonsai, trained in the traditional candle flame style, shows the formation of "Chi Chi", which are strange, thickened, pendulous growths at the junctions of the branches and trunk. These develop on old ginkgos both as bonsai and in the wild.

The tree was purchased a few years ago. The author was not happy about it and examination showed that part of the main trunk was rotting, possibly through age, a theory reinforced by the presence of the Chi Chi. The following spring, a few shoots of a suspect branch had died back and were removed, and though the remainder of the branch came into leaf it lacked vigour. However, shoots from the surrounding branches were encouraged to fill the space and all was considered well.

The following year, in spring, shortly before the leaves opened, the bonsai was taken out of London to spend the summer in as near a perfect environment as possible. On arrival it was found that the suspect branch had fallen off, and this unlikely happening revealed the true nature of the tree. It was indeed old, probably very old, and at some stage had suffered an accident causing it to lose part of its centre. Probably it had been broken in some way, and with great skill, the broken branches had been grafted into the remains of the old trunk and these grafts had, for a time, been successful. However, the passing of the years and a period of neglect had caused dieback of the old trunk which carried the grafts, one of which had, because of this, now fallen off. Currently the tree is being trained in anticipation of other grafts falling away. It is likely that in due course the centre of the tree will die completely, necessitating considerable branch growth from the healthy parts remaining.

The grafted branch was already weak before it fell, but attempts were made to root it in a well-equipped propagating house. Hope was almost gone when a green bud was seen, and a few days later the entire branch came into leaf. Now, this piece of the old tree is firmly established on its own roots.

Despite its problems, this is still a magnificent old bonsai, and is currently potted in a rectangular kataoka pot of 19 in by 13¾ in by 3¾ in (47.5 cm by 34.5 cm by 9.5 cm) having an overall height of 33 in (83 cm), and a trunk girth of 20½ in (51 cm).

Unlike all but one other of the bonsai illustrated in colour in the book, this tree has not yet been given a personal name by the author.

LEFT: *A 14-year-old mame* Cotoneaster horizontalis, *5in (13cm) tall.*

RIGHT: *A fine old double, red-flowered hawthorn* (Crataegus monogyna) *trained as a bonsai for many years.*

Crassula sarcocaulis Half-hardy evergreen. Flowering. This plant forms an attractive, small, flowering bonsai with a well-branched frame and narrow, fleshy leaves. The flower buds are red, opening to clusters of pink flowers in August. These smell unpleasantly. There is a white-flowered form, *C. sarcocaulis alba.*

Propagation	Cuttings.
CULTURAL NEEDS	
Re-potting	Every two years in April, using the coniferous mixture.
Pruning	Trim as necessary during the growing season.
Wiring	Do not wire.
Fertiliser	Apply May to September, sparingly.
Pests	Generally trouble-free.
NOTE	Protect from excessive winter wet.

Crataegus monogyna (hawthorn, may tree) Hardy, deciduous. Flowering. Ideal for many styles of bonsai with its finely-branched growth, small-lobed and toothed dark green leaves; attractive clusters of sweet-smelling flowers in May and red berries in autumn.

Propagation	Seeds (slow to germinate).
CULTURAL NEEDS	
Re-potting	Once every two years. March.
Pruning	July and August.
Wiring	During summer months on young wood.
Fertiliser	Apply in April and September.

Pests and Diseases Generally free of pests but may develop powdery mildew in a wet summer.

NOTE   There are other crataegus species and hybrids and most are suitable for bonsai training.

Cryptomeria japonica (Japanese cedar) Hardy conifer. Easily grown conifer with awl-shaped leaves turning bronze-red in autumn. Very suitable for training in the formal upright style.

Propagation   Seeds or cuttings.

CULTURAL NEEDS

Re-potting   Once every two to four years in April, using the coniferous compost mixture. Avoid re-potting earlier.

Pruning   Nip buds as they develop to maintain good shape and dense bushy growth.

Wiring   Do not wire.

Fertiliser   Apply in April or May and in autumn.

Pests   Generally trouble-free.

Daphne retusa Hardy evergreen. Flowering. This attractive alpine shrub has lustrous, dark green, obovate leaves, and rose-purple flowers which are

An aged Cryptomeria japonica *trained in the formal style. A vigorous grower, pruned every few days throughout the summer.*

borne in clusters on terminal shoots in May and June. It can be trained to form an interesting small bonsai of informal style.

Propagation   Seeds or cuttings.

CULTURAL NEEDS

Re-potting   Every two years in March in standard mixture.
Pruning   Immediately after flowering as required.
Wiring   Summer.
Fertiliser   Apply from May to September, monthly.
Pests   Generally trouble-free.

Diospyros kaki (persimmon) Half-hardy, deciduous, flowering and fruiting. Not an easy tree to train, but worth the effort should it fruit. It needs winter protection and plenty of water and fertiliser.

Propagation   Seeds.

CULTURAL NEEDS

Re-potting   Every three or four years in early spring, taking care not to damage the roots.
Pruning   In early spring before buds appear.
Wiring   Carefully, in early summer, with protected wire.
Fertiliser   Apply generously until flowering, then very moderately until fruit has formed, after which increase again.
Pests   Relatively trouble-free.
NOTE   Protect from cold and frost in winter.

Elaeagnus umbellata Hardy, deciduous. This vigorous shrub can be trained into informal upright styles. Foliage is dark green above, silvery underneath, and the plant carries attractive cream-white flowers on its branches in May, followed by round red fruits.

Propagation   Seeds.

CULTURAL NEEDS

Re-potting   Every other year in March, using the standard compost mixture.
Pruning   After flowering.
Wiring   Rarely needed.
Fertiliser   Apply occasionally during growing season.
Pests   Generally trouble-free.

Euonymus alatus (winged spindle) Hardy, deciduous, flowering and fruiting. Grown for its autumn foliage colour, which rivals that of the maple, and its clusters of berries. It also has interesting bark, giving yet another feature of interest.

Propagation   Seeds, cuttings.

CULTURAL NEEDS

Re-potting   Late March or early April, once every two to three years, using the standard compost mixture with a little added loam.
Pruning   Before spring, when the buds appear.
Wiring   During early summer.

Fertiliser	Apply generously, during the summer months.
Pests	Generally trouble-free.
NOTE	Very sensitive to cold spells in winter and equally sensitive to summer drought.

Euonymus japonicus (Japanese spindle tree) Almost hardy evergreen. Little seen as bonsai in Britain but frequently used in Japan, it has leathery, very shiny foliage and 2 in (5 cm) long cymes of greenish-white flowers in May and June. Sometimes the brilliant orange berries are seen in autumn.

Propagation	Seeds or cuttings.

CULTURAL NEEDS

Re-potting	Annually in March.
Pruning	Shorten non-flowering branches.
Wiring	Do not wire.
Fertiliser	Occasionally, with fertiliser high in potash and phosphate.
Pests	Generally trouble-free.
NOTE	There are both evergreen and deciduous species of spindle and many are amenable to training. Deciduous kinds are hardier than those which are evergreen.

Fagus sylvatica (beech) Hardy, deciduous. An easy and very attractive tree to grow. It is suited to most bonsai styles. Very pleasing autumn colouring and holds its dead leaves in winter.

Propagation	Seeds.

CULTURAL NEEDS

Re-potting	Every one to two years, using the standard compost mixture.
Pruning	Remove unwanted young growth when it develops.
Wiring	Try to avoid.
Fertiliser	Apply a little occasionally, during the growing season.
Pests	Occasionally troubled with whitefly.
NOTE	*Fagus sylvatica purpurea* (copper beech), *F. s. heterophylla* (syn. *F. s. asplenifolia*, fern-leaved beech) and *F. crenata* (Japanese white beech) are all suited to bonsai cultivation. Needs as above.

Ficus benjamina (weeping fig) Tender evergreen. Reminiscent of a birch tree with camellia-like foliage, this ficus can be trained as an attractive indoor bonsai in informal upright style.

Propagation	Seeds, cuttings, air-layers.

CULTURAL NEEDS

Re-potting	Every one or two years in April or May, using the standard compost mixture.
Pruning	Pinch back young shoots.
Wiring	Do not use.
Fertiliser	Apply from May to September.
Pests	Scale insect, mealy bug, red spider mite.
NOTE	Likes light position but not constant, direct sunshine.

*A beech (*Fagus sylvatica*) trained in the windswept style. It was collected about 17 years ago and is now over 30 years old.*

Ficus macrophylla (Moreton Bay fig) Tender evergreen. This ficus grows, even when quite young, a bulbous base to its trunk. As it matures aerial roots are produced from the branches. Easily grown indoors, it makes a most unusual, upright, informal bonsai with dark green, shiny, camellia-like foliage.
Propagation   Seeds, cuttings.
CULTURAL NEEDS As for *F. benjamina.*

Ficus pumila Half-hardy evergreen. This small-leaved ficus has a growth habit like ivy, climbing and trailing and makes a attractive small or mame bonsai for the home.
Propagation   Cuttings.
CULTURAL NEEDS As for *Ficus benjamina.*

Ficus radicans variegata Tender evergreen. Another small-leaved ficus with attractive creamy-white edged leaves that, though trailing by nature, responds to training as a small, informal upright, indoor bonsai.
Propagation   Cuttings.
CULTURAL NEEDS As for *F. benjamina.*

Forsythia Hardy, deciduous. Flowering. Easily grown and very worthwhile as an informal upright bonsai for its magnificent display of bright yellow flowers in March and April.

Propagation   Cuttings.

CULTURAL NEEDS

Re-potting   Annually or every two years after flowering, using the standard compost mixture.

Pruning   Immediately after flowering.

Wiring   Do not wire.

Fertiliser   Apply a little from May to September.

Pests   Generally trouble-free.

Fraxinus excelsior (common ash) Hardy, deciduous. This vigorously growing tree with pinnate leaves forms an attractive informal upright bonsai, which has an attractive look in winter with its black buds and silver bark.

Propagation   Seeds.

CULTURAL NEEDS

Re-potting   Once every two years in March, using the standard compost mixture.

Pruning   In summer prune shoots. Apical buds may be removed in December to encourage a more branched habit.

Wiring   During summer; wire-marks easily.

Fertiliser   Apply from May to September, sparingly.

Pests   Generally trouble-free.

Fuchsia magellanica pumila Hardy, deciduous. Flowering. This, the hardiest of the fuchsias, is delightful to train as an informal upright or broom-style bonsai. Small leaves, twiggy growth habit and many small red flowers in summer, make this a most rewarding shrub to train. As a bonsai it must be protected from cold and wet in winter.

Propagation   Cuttings.

CULTURAL NEEDS

Re-potting   Annually in March, using the standard compost mixture.

Pruning   Prune hard in March. Subsequently nip out young shoots as required until late June.

Wiring   Do not wire.

Fertiliser   Feed weekly with dilute liquid fertiliser throughout growing season.

Pests   Generally trouble-free.

Ginkgo biloba (maidenhair tree) Hardy, deciduous conifer. *Ginkgo biloba* is traditionally trained in candle-flame style, a varient of the upright style. The ginkgo has magnificent autumn colour – a clear yellow though lasting only a few days – and opens its leaves very late in spring.

Propagation   Seeds (with difficulty), cuttings.

CULTURAL NEEDS

Re-potting   Annually in late March, using coniferous compost mixture.

Pruning   Prune long shoots as they grow.

Wiring	Branches in March, young shoots in early summer.
Fertiliser	Regular fertiliser required throughout the growing season.
Pests	Generally trouble-free.
NOTE	The variegated form, if obtainable, is also of interest.

Hedera helix (common ivy) Hardy evergreen. Formerly rarely seen, but in recent years this is growing in popularity as bonsai in a variety of styles. There is a wide choice of cultivars of *Hedera helix* and all can be trained. Most tolerate some sun or shade.

Propagation	Cuttings.
CULTURAL NEEDS	
Re-potting	Annually in April, using the standard compost mixture.
Pruning	Remove long shoots during the growing season, leaf-prune in July.
Wiring	Do not wire.
Fertiliser	Do not use.
Pests	Scale insect, occasionally.

Ilex aquifolium (holly) Hardy evergreen. An unusual tree as a bonsai, but can be trained in various informal upright styles.

Propagation	Cuttings.
CULTURAL NEEDS	
Re-potting	Re-pot every two years in April, using the standard compost mixture.
Pruning	Prune shoots as they grow. Leaf-prune in July.
Wiring	Wire young shoots before they become woody. Wire-marks easily.
Fertiliser	Apply in April or May and in autumn.
Pests	Scale insect. Holly leaf miner (cut off affected leaves).

Jasminum nudiflorum (winter jasmine) Hardy, deciduous. Flowering. This is primarily trained for the beauty of its small, clear yellow flowers, which open in spring before the leaves.

Propagation	Cuttings.
CULTURAL NEEDS	
Re-potting	Once every year or two years, immediately after flowers fall, using the standard compost mixture.
Pruning	Trim after flowering.
Wiring	In winter, on old wood. New season's growth in September.
Fertiliser	Commence feeding one month after re-potting and feed until April and again in September and October.
Pests	Generally trouble-free.

Juniperus chinensis (Chinese juniper) Hardy conifer. One of the classical bonsai species and suitable for training in all ways.

Propagation	Cuttings.

CULTURAL NEEDS

Re-potting	Every two or three years, late autumn or early spring in the coniferous compost mixture.
Pruning	Pinch out shooting buds while soft.
Wiring	Winter.
Fertiliser	Apply between March and May and in autumn.
Pests	Red spider mite.

Juniperus communis (common juniper) Hardy conifer. The native European juniper has juvenile foliage (needles) and can be trained in a similar fashion to *J. rigida*.

Propagation	Seeds or cuttings.
CULTURAL NEEDS	As for *J. rigida*.

Juniperus rigida ssp. **nipponica** (needle juniper) Hardy conifer. Again, a very popular bonsai in Japan and used for almost every style.

Propagation	Cuttings.

CULTURAL NEEDS

Re-potting	Every three years in April, using the coniferous compost mixture.
Pruning	Pinch out buds while still soft. Remove buds in June if tree is healthy.
Wiring	October to April.
Fertiliser	Apply in spring and autumn.
Pests	Red spider mite.
NOTE	The form of this juniper which is obtained from Japan as *Juniperus rigida* is, in the author's experience, more likely to be *J. rigida* ssp. *nipponica* which is prostrate and has more glaucous, shorter-needled foliage than the species.

Laburnum anagyroides (golden rain tree) Hardy deciduous. Flowering. The common laburnum is an easily-grown tree, normally seen in informal upright or sloping trunk styles that show off its pendulous racemes of bright yellow flowers. These are a magnificent sight in early June.

Propagation	Seeds.

CULTURAL NEEDS

Re-potting	Annually in spring in standard mixture.
Pruning	After flowering.
Wiring	In summer; wire-marks easily.
Fertiliser	Apply after flowering and in autumn with high phosphate fertiliser.
Pests	Generally trouble-free.

Larix decidua (European larch) Hardy, deciduous conifer. Most of the larches are eminently suited to bonsai training in formal and informal upright; sloping trunk; windswept, and the various multiple trunk styles. They are very graceful trees, with their spring foliage a soft green, whilst in autumn this changes to a golden russet hue. The larches will flower and cone from a very early age, and hold old cones for up to four years.

Propagation   Seeds.

CULTURAL NEEDS

Re-potting   Every two years in March, using the coniferous compost mixture.

Pruning   Nip back soft young growth as it appears.

Wiring   Winter; wire-marks easily.

Fertiliser   Apply in April, May and September.

Pests   Generally trouble-free.

Leptospermum scoparium (manuka) Half-hardy evergreen. Flowering. This little-known, New Zealand shrub, has great potential for training in a number of bonsai styles. It has small, dark green, narrow leaves and flowers freely in May and June. The species has white flowers but named varieties offer pink, crimson and double ones of deep red and rose-pink.

Propagation   Cuttings.

CULTURAL NEEDS

Re-potting   In April every second year, using the standard compost mixture.

Pruning   Branch pruning in April. Nip shoots as they grow to encourage branching and maintain shape.

Wiring   No wiring.

Fertiliser   Apply in April and September.

Pests   Generally trouble-free.

Liquidambar styraciflua (sweet gum) Hardy, deciduous. These trees can be trained in the manner of Japanese maples (*Acer palmatum* varieties). Indeed the foliage is very like that of the maples and has the same intense autumn colouring. As the trees mature a corky bark develops.

Propagation   Seeds.

CULTURAL NEEDS

Re-potting   Every one or two years in April, using the standard compost mixture.

Pruning   Nip growing shoots in spring and summer.

Wiring   Early summer with caution.

Fertiliser   Apply between May and September.

Pests   Generally trouble-free.

Malus baccata (crab apple) Hardy deciduous. Flowering. There are many species, hybrids and varieties of crab apple and most of them are easily trained to informal upright bonsai. Preferably, select small-fruited varieties.

Propagation   Seeds, grafting.

CULTURAL NEEDS

Re-potting   Once yearly in March in standard mixture.

Pruning   Trim after flowering. Shorten long branches after June.

Wiring   Old branches in winter, new growth in June.

Fertiliser   Apply once before flowering, again in September.

Pests and Diseases Aphids, mildew.

Malus halliana Hardy, deciduous. Flowering. A crab apple suited for use as a mame bonsai as well as in other styles.

Propagation	Seeds, grafting.

CULTURAL NEEDS

Re-potting	Every two years in late March. It is essential to do this if the specimen is pot-bound. Re-potting can also be carrried out in September if the plant is subsequently fed.
Pruning	Lightly, in summer.
Wiring	Summer.
Fertiliser	Apply before flowering and in late summer.
Pests and Diseases	Aphids, mildew.
NOTE	Avoid damaging bark.

Metasequoia glyptostroboides (dawn redwood) Hardy, deciduous conifer. A very graceful tree of beautiful colour. The young growth is light green and changes to pink, then red and brown, before dropping in mid-November. Now becoming quite widely planted in Britain, this fossil-age conifer, re-discovered in a remote part of China in 1941, shows great potential for upright styles of planting and responds to training.

Propagation	Cuttings.

CULTURAL NEEDS

Re-potting	Every second year in late March, using coniferous compost mixture.
Pruning	Nip growing shoots as they lengthen.
Wiring	October and May.
Fertiliser	Apply in April, May and autumn.
Pests	Generally trouble-free.
NOTE	As a bonsai, this tree should have winter protection in a cold frame or in similar conditions.

Morus nigra (black mulberry) Hardy, deciduous. Occasionally grown as small, informal upright bonsai, this creates considerable interest. The leaves reduce well and they have an attractive form.

Propagation	Cuttings.

CULTURAL NEEDS

Re-potting	Once every two years in late March, using standard compost mixture.
Pruning	Nip back new shoots as required. Avoid pruning large branches.
Wiring	Avoid wiring.
Fertiliser	Apply in April and September.
Pests	Generally trouble-free.

Parthenocissus inserta Hardy, deciduous. Surprising though it may seem, this climber, which is a near relative of the Virginia creeper, makes a good informal-style bonsai. It is a magnificent sight when the foliage colours in autumn, before falling, and with bonsai training seems to have a noticeable red tint during the summer.

Propagation	Seeds, cuttings.
CULTURAL NEEDS	
Re-potting	In late March annually or every other year, using standard mixture.
Pruning	Trim back climbing shoots to one or two leaves in late spring or summer.
Wiring	No wiring.
Fertiliser	Apply in April and autumn.
Pests	Scale insects, aphids, red spider mite.

Parthenocissus quinquefolia Virginia creeper (treat as for *P. inserta).*

Phoenix canariensis (Canary Islands palm) Tender, evergreen. Palms can be trained as bonsai and look attractive as indoor bonsai.

Propagation	Seeds.
CULTURAL NEEDS	
Re-potting	Annually in April or May, using coniferous compost mixture.
Pruning	None required.
Wiring	None required.
Fertiliser	Apply at the end of May and in August and September.
Pests	Scale insects, occasionally.
NOTE	The date palm, *P. dactylifera*, requires similar cultivation.

Picea glehnii (sakhalin spruce) Hardy conifer. A popular, dense growing spruce, much used for bonsai because, unlike many members of the genus *Picea* it is comparitively tolerant of soot and dust pollution.

Propagation	Cuttings, grafting, layering.
CULTURAL NEEDS	
Re-potting	Every five years to six years in spring or early autumn, using coniferous mixture and extra leaf-mould.
Pruning	New growth should be pinched back in late September.
Wiring	December to February, avoiding frosty spells.
Fertiliser	Lightly in spring and late summer.
Pests	Relatively trouble-free.

Picea jezoensis (yezo spruce) Hardy, conifer. This very attractive, densely-branched spruce is rarely seen as a bonsai in the United Kingdom, perhaps due to the long-standing ban on its import from Japan. Lack of examples has probably inhibited the use of other piceas as bonsai. Several are worth training and would result in trees suitable for group or rock planting as well as individually trained bonsai in most upright styles.

Propagation	Seeds.
CULTURAL NEEDS	
Re-potting	Once every four to six years, using coniferous compost mixture.
Pruning	Nip shoots in June or July.
Wiring	October until following April.

Pinus parviflora, *an ideal conifer for planting on slate or stone.*

Fertiliser   Apply regularly from April to November.
Pests   Red spider mite.

Pinus densiflora (Japanese red pine) Hardy conifer. This elegant tree is, alas, rarely seen in the United Kingdom, but it is a species which can be readily grown from seed. It is a conifer which responds well to bonsai training in all styles.

Propagation   Seeds.
CULTURAL NEEDS
Re-potting   Once every four to five years, in March or April, using the coniferous compost mixture.
Pruning   Nip out buds before they develop.
Wiring   October until following April.
Fertiliser   Apply in spring and autumn.
Pests   Woolly aphid.

Pinus parviflora (Japanese white pine)
P. sylvestris (Scots pine)
P. thunbergii (Japanese black pine)
P. thunbergii var. **corticata** (Japanese brocade pine)
These are all treated in a similar fashion to *Pinus densiflora*, bud nipping on *P. parviflora* being only for the removal of extra-long growth.

Platanus x hispanica (London plane) Hardy, deciduous. When trained as an informal upright bonsai, the leaves resemble those of a maple. Trunk peels characteristically in older trees.

Propagation	Seeds.
CULTURAL NEEDS	
Re-potting	Every two to three years in late March, using the standard compost mixture.
Pruning	Nip back developing shoots. Leaf-prune in July.
Wiring	In summer.
Fertiliser	Apply in May and September.
Pests	Relatively trouble-free.

Podocarpus macrophyllus (Kusamaki) Hardy in milder parts of Britain; conifer. There are several *Podocarpus* available and as a group they respond well to bonsai training. As bonsai they should have winter protection.

Propagation	Cuttings.
CULTURAL NEEDS	
Re-potting	Every three or four years, using the coniferous compost mixture.
Pruning	Any time except winter.
Wiring	Autumn and winter.
Fertiliser	Apply in spring and autumn.
Pests	Generally trouble-free.

Populus alba (white poplar) Hardy, deciduous. The poplar makes an attractive informal upright bonsai.

Propagation	Cuttings or suckers
CULTURAL NEEDS	
Re-potting	Annually, in late March, using the standard compost mixture.
Pruning	Prune back young shoots in summer.
Wiring	In summer, if needed.
Fertiliser	Apply in May and September.
Pests	Relatively trouble-free.
NOTE	There are many varieties of poplar suited to bonsai training.

Prunus avium (gean) Hardy, deciduous. Flowering. Grown for flowers and fruit with fine autumn colour an extra. Delightful and informal-style bonsai.

Propagation	Seeds.
CULTURAL NEEDS	
Re-potting	Annually, in October, using the standard compost mixture.

Pruning   After flowering.
Wiring   In winter; use plastic-coated wire.
Fertiliser   Apply in spring and autumn.
Pests   Finches and tits.

Prunus dulcis (common almond) Hardy, deciduous. Flowering. A tree grown for its pink blossoms, it has finer foliage than other members of the genus *Prunus* and responds to training.
Propagation   Seeds.
CULTURAL NEEDS As for *Prunus avium*.
Pests and Diseases Finches, tits and peach leaf curl.

Prunus mume (Japanese flowering apricot) Hardy, deciduous. Flowering. Again, grown for its flowers, which are very sweet-scented and produced very early in the year. There are white or pink forms and all are attractive.
Propagation   Seed, grafting.
CULTURAL NEEDS
Re-potting   Late spring, annually, using the standard compost mixture.
Pruning   Immediately after flowering and again after new shoots are produced.
Wiring   In summer; use plastic-coated wire.
Fertiliser   Apply in spring, summer and autumn.
Pests   Generally trouble-free.
NOTE   Give some protection in winter.

Prunus persica (peach) Hardy, deciduous. Flowering. Examples seen in Britain are usually imported, grafted plants. Attractive while flowering, their large leaves make them of less interest for the rest of the year.
Propagation   Seeds, grafting.
CULTURAL NEEDS
Re-potting   Annually, after flowering, using the standard compost mixture.
Pruning   After flowering and in summer.
Wiring   In summer. Use plastic-coated wire.
Fertiliser   Apply lightly, before flowering, and in September.
Diseases   Peach leaf curl.

Punica granatum (pomegranate) Tender, deciduous. An attractive bonsai with small, shiny leaves, tinged red when opening, clearing to bright green. Autumn colour is a clear yellow. Will carry its brilliant red flowers in years when the springs are long, warm and sunny. Fruit is rarely carried in Britain.
Propagation   Seeds, cuttings.
CULTURAL NEEDS
Re-potting   In May, once every two years, using the standard compost mixture.
Pruning   In summer.
Wiring   In summer.
Fertiliser   Apply occasionally, during growing season, using a ferti-

liser with a high phosphate content.

Pests Scale insects.

Pyracantha angustifolia (firethorn) Hardy evergreen. Flowering. Widely grown and trained for its clusters of white flowers in May or June and the orange-yellow berries which are carried profusely in the autumn. The foliage is small, dark and shiny and the overall effect is very attractive. Many forms exist with orange and red berries, all suitable for training.

Propagation Seeds, cuttings.

CULTURAL NEEDS

Re-potting Every other year, in spring, using the standard compost mixture.

Pruning After flowering (summer).

Wiring Summer.

Fertiliser Apply in spring and high phosphate fertiliser in autumn.

Pests Generally trouble-free.

Pyrus communis (pear) Hardy, deciduous, flowering. Easily grown and suited to informal upright training, the pear tree is grown for its white, early-summer blossoms.

Propagation Seeds, grafting.

CULTURAL NEEDS

Re-potting Annually in late March, using the standard compost mixture.

Pruning Shorten long branches in winter, leaving flowering spurs.

Wiring Do not wire.

Fertiliser Apply once in April, then monthly after fruits have set.

Pests Spray with a winter wash (suitable for fruit trees) to avoid trouble from pests.

Quercus ilex (holm oak) Hardy, evergreen. Easier to train than the common oak (see below), the holm oak has very dark foliage, contrasting vividly with silvery new growth.

Propagation as for *Q. robur.*

CULTURAL NEEDS as for *Q. robur.*

Pests as for *Q. robur.*

NOTE There are many varieties of oak growing in Britain. Select acorns for seed from a tree that has smaller-than-average foliage or a better-than-average autumn colour.

Quercus robur (common oak) Hardy, deciduous. Slow growing but interesting to train, this very British tree becomes attractive in four to five years and can be further developed to become a fine informal upright bonsai.

Propagation Seeds.

CULTURAL NEEDS

Re-potting Every two years in early April, using the standard compost mixture.

Pruning Remove apical buds in December to encourage lateral growth. Trim young shoots in summer.

Wiring	Young shoots in summer.
Fertiliser	Apply in May and September.
Pests and Diseases	Oak galls, mildew.

Rhus succedanea (wax tree) Hardy, deciduous. Prized for its foliage colour in autumn, the wax tree responds readily to pruning. Some people are allergic to substances contained within this tree so it should be handled with caution.

Propagation	Seeds.

CULTURAL NEEDS

Re-potting	If kept well fed, this tree needs re-potting only once every two or three years, using the standard compost mixture with added loam.
Pruning	Spring or summer.
Wiring	Summer.
Fertiliser	Apply regularly, in spring and autumn.
Pests	Relatively trouble-free.
NOTE	Handle with care (see opening remarks above). This tree must not be allowed to become dry in winter.

Salix babylonica (weeping willow) Hardy, deciduous. This species forms a most attractive tree in the weeping branch style. Fast-growing and easily trained, an impressive bonsai can be achieved within a few years.

Propagation	Cuttings.

CULTURAL NEEDS

Re-potting	Twice a year, in early April and August, using the standard compost mixture.
Pruning	In the growing season; remove buds or shoots on underside of the branches.
Wiring	Rarely necessary; bend with fingers.
Fertiliser	Apply in late spring and September.
Pests	Caterpillars, in summer.
NOTE	There are many other species and varieties of *Salix* and almost all are suited to bonsai training. The pruning of upright varieties is normally carried out in summer, following the growth of shoots.

Sequoia sempervirens (redwood) Hardy conifer. A tree of the largest size in its native habitat, this is, nevertheless, amenable to training as a small or large bonsai in upright styles.

Propagation	Seeds.

CULTURAL NEEDS

Re-potting	Every other year, in early April, using the coniferous compost mixture.
Pruning	Nip developing shoots in late spring and summer.
Wiring	In summer, if necessary.
Fertiliser	Apply in May and September.

| *Pests* | Generally trouble-free. |
| NOTE | The giant redwood, *Sequoiadendron giganteum*, is also recommended, and its cultural needs are as for *S. sempervirens*. |

Sophora japonica (Japanese pagoda tree) Hardy, deciduous. A pinnate-leaved tree which makes a pretty bonsai once branching structure created.
Propagation   Seeds.
CULTURAL NEEDS

Re-potting	Every other year, in early April, using the standard compost mixture.
Pruning	Remove apex and leaf-prune in June.
Wiring	In summer; wire-marks easily.
Fertiliser	Apply in May and September.
Pests	Scale insects, occasionally.

Sorbus aucuparia (rowan or mountain ash) Hardy, deciduous. This delightful tree is a popular small bonsai in Britain. Easily grown, it is especially attractive in autumn, its pinnate, serrated leaves turning to rich shades of red.
Propagation   Seeds.
CULTURAL NEEDS

Re-potting	Every other year in March, using the standard compost mixture.
Pruning	Trim young shoots as necessary during the summer; leaf-prune in July.
Wiring	In summer, if required.
Fertiliser	Apply in spring and autumn, sparingly.
Pests	Generally trouble-free.

Spiraea japonica Hardy, deciduous. Flowering. This popular garden shrub is rewarding to train as a mame or small bonsai.
Propagation   Seeds, cuttings.
CULTURAL NEEDS

Re-potting	Every other year, in March, using the standard compost mixture.
Pruning	Nip back shoots in early summer. Remove long, thick, straight shoots which occasionally develop.
Wiring	Not needed.
Fertiliser	Apply in May and September.
Pests	Generally trouble-free.
NOTE	Many other spiraeas are worth cultivating as bonsai.

Syringa vulgaris (lilac) Hardy, deciduous. Flowering. An easy tree to train, with attractive, heart-shaped, mid-green leaves.
Propagation   Cuttings, suckers.
CULTURAL NEEDS

| *Re-potting* | Every other year in March, using the standard compost mixture. |

Pruning	Remove leading buds in December to encourage branching. Otherwise trim shoots as required in summer.
Wiring	Not needed.
Fertiliser	Apply in April and September.
Pests	Generally trouble-free.

Tamarix pentandra (tamarisk) Hardy, deciduous. Flowering. Like the weeping willow, the tamarisk is usually trained as an upright or sloping-trunk weeping tree. It bears very attractive, feathery, pink flowers in August.

Propagation	Cuttings.
CULTURAL NEEDS	
Re-potting	Every other year, in April, using the standard compost mixture.
Pruning	Between October and February.
Wiring	In winter.
Fertiliser	Apply in May and September.
Pests	Generally trouble-free.

Taxodium distichum (swamp cypress) Hardy, deciduous conifer. In nature it is a large tree with attractive fine, yew-like foliage that turns brilliant golden-red in autumn. It is suitable for upright styles and can be stood in water.

Propagation	Seeds, cuttings.
CULTURAL NEEDS	
Re-potting	Every other year, in late April, using the coniferous compost mixture.
Pruning	Cut off unwanted buds in June; new shoots should be nipped back in July and August.
Wiring	In summer, if needed.
Fertiliser	Apply in April and September.
Pests	Scale insects.

Taxus baccata (yew) Hardy conifer. Well-known, slow-growing tree, of interest to bonsai growers. It is attractive in upright styles.

Propagation	Seeds, cuttings.
CULTURAL NEEDS	
Re-potting	Every one or two years, using the standard compost mixture.
Pruning	Trim new shoots in May and August.
Wiring	In summer, if needed.
Fertiliser	Apply in April and September.
Pests	Scale insects.
NOTE	Poisonous in all its parts.

Tilia cordata (small-leaved lime) Hardy, deciduous. Leaf size reduces dramatically on this lime, making it a worthwhile tree as an informal upright bonsai.

Propagation	Seeds.

CULTURAL NEEDS

Re-potting	Every other year, in late March, using the standard compost mixture.
Pruning	Trim shoots in June and July.
Wiring	In summer.
Fertiliser	Apply in May and September.
Pests	Usually trouble-free.

Trachycarpus fortunei (Chusan palm) Fairly hardy, evergreen. This makes an amusing addition to a collection and is easy to cultivate in a pot.

Propagation Seeds or basal suckers.

CULTURAL NEEDS

Re-potting	Annually in April or May, using the coniferous compost mixture.
Pruning	None required.
Wiring	None required.
Fertiliser	Apply at the end of May and in August-September.
Pests	Scale insects.

Tsuga heterophylla (western hemlock) Hardy conifer. Another conifer suitable for formal or informal upright training, as is its near relative, the eastern hemlock, *T. canadensis*.

Propagation Seeds, cuttings.

CULTURAL NEEDS

Re-potting	Once every three years, between March and May, using the coniferous compost mixture.
Pruning	Nip back buds and/or young shoots between May and July. Trim branches in October.
Wiring	Not usually required, but can be used in October.
Fertiliser	Apply in spring, June and October.
Pests	Generally trouble-free.

Ulmus parvifolia (Chinese elm) Hardy, deciduous. Popular for its tiny leaves and corky bark, this trains well into most bonsai styles.

Propagation Cuttings.

CULTURAL NEEDS

Re-potting	Every second year, in March, using the standard compost mixture.
Pruning	Nip new shoots in early summer, leaf-prune in July.
Wiring	In summer; wire-marks easily.
Fertiliser	Apply in spring and autumn.
Pests and Diseases	Generally trouble-free as far as pests are concerned; susceptible to Dutch elm disease.

Ulmus procera (English elm) Hardy, deciduous. Elms make attractive bonsai and are especially valued in areas where Dutch elm disease has killed all others.

Propagation Suckers and layers.

CULTURAL NEEDS As for *U. parvifolia*.

*A Chinese elm (*Ulmus parvifolia*) trained in the sloping trunk style. This tree, imported in 1972, is undergoing extensive retraining; the heavy, upper left-hand branch will shortly be removed and the crown lowered by some 4in (10cm).*

Wisteria floribunda Hardy, deciduous climber. Flowering. Grown for its racemes of flowers. A good-sized, shapely wisteria bonsai in full bloom is an inspiring sight.

Propagation	Cuttings, grafts, layers, seed.

CULTURAL NEEDS

Re-potting	In early March, using the standard compost mixture.
Pruning	Prune hard, in February.
Wiring	In summer, if required.
Fertiliser	Apply in April and September.
Pests	Scale insects.

Zelkova serrata Hardy, deciduous. Zelkovas are related to the elms, and *Zelkova serrata* is a justifiably popular species both in Britain and Japan. Suitable for informal upright, broom or group planting styles, and also as a mame bonsai. It is easy to grow, responds very well to pruning, and provides a bonus in the form of excellent autumn foliage colour.

Propagation	Seeds, cuttings.

CULTURAL NEEDS

Re-potting	Every other year, in late March, using the standard compost mixture.
Pruning	Any time.
Wiring	Not advisable as it marks the bark.
Fertiliser	Apply in spring and autumn.
Pests	Scale insects, aphids.

APPENDIX A

OVERWINTERING BONSAI IN DIFFICULT CLIMATES

The overwintering of bonsai in Britain has already been discussed in Chapter 4 (see p. 45 and p. 46) but there will be those readers whose climatic conditions preclude the use of the comparitively simple methods of winter care recommended.

If you live in an area where the winters are long and constantly below freezing, there will be difficulties if your collection is a large one, but if the collection is small there is a very simple method of protection whereby bonsai which would perish out of doors can be kept safely all winter. Moreover, it has the added advantage that the trees can be checked regularly without discomfort. They do, of course, need the dormant rest period that would occur naturally in other conditions, and most bonsai hardy in Britain overwinter comfortably in temperatures of 35° to 40°F (2 to 4.5°C). This, by good fortune, is the usual temperature of a domestic refrigerator, and trees can be placed in their pots in one of these at the onset of winter. Deciduous trees will be bare of leaves and the darkness will have little effect on them, while coniferous trees do not seem adversely affected, provided they are shaded for a few days in spring when brought out into the open again. About once every 10 days the trees should be checked to make sure they are not drying out, for evaporation takes place, even in a refrigerator. Should they need watering, remove them and water moderately, waiting a few hours before replacing them in the refrigerator. In spring, the trees may be taken outside once more when the danger of severe frosts occuring is past, and within a short time growth will start.

Some bonsai specimens may begin making new leaves in the refrigerator before it is possible to put them outside. One of the earliest to come into growth under these conditions is the crab apple, which can form very early flower buds. Especial care should be taken not to expose such trees to difficult conditions such as strong sunshine or sudden frosts when they are first taken outside. In warm climates the refrigerator technique can be used to enable collectors to cultivate temperate climate trees. These bonsai also need a period of dormancy which can be induced by progressively longer stays in the refrigerator. When leaves have dropped, the trees can be refrigerated for a month before being brought out to commence their spring growth.

For the owners of larger collections who live in areas where the winters are prolonged and severe, two other methods of overwintering are suggested. The first requires the use of a garden shed of appropriate size. This should be well made and its walls and roof lined with a suitable form of insulating material such as fibreboard. Windows, other than north-facing ones (in the northern hemisphere) should also be covered, all of which is intended to produce a storage place which is not subject to sudden temperature fluctuations, either downward or upwards. Even winter sun, shining through glass, can raise the temperature inside a shed to almost tropical warmth.

Staging and shelving should be erected of suitable size and strength. Slatted staging, if correctly built, is economical of materials and able to carry considerable weights. Vertical planking should then be fixed around the edges of the staging, as is done with that used for alpine plants, the pots of which are plunged to their rims in gravel. A box-like bench top will have been formed, and sheets of polystyrene can be laid on the slats, the small gaps between them being sufficient for drainage purposes.

On top of this add a ½ in (1 cm) layer of polystyrene chips and the area is ready for bonsai to be positioned. Once these are in place, more polystyrene chips can be added to fill up spaces in between pots and as a covering over them, a depth of 4 to 6 in (10 to 15 cm) being necessary, which is retained in place by the vertical planking. A maximum-minimum thermometer should be installed and the trees checked weekly to see if they need watering. In regions where experience indicates the possibility of periods of prolonged temperatures below 23°F (−5°C), suitable heaters should also be used. The simplest and most efficient ones are probably thermostatically controlled tubular electric heaters, which can be installed around the shed below the staging. This will ensure circulation of air, to the benefit of the bonsai. The thermostat should be set at 34° to 35°F(1° to 2°C),and to economise on running costs, windows should be fitted with wooden shutters which may be closed during the coldest period of winter. In addition to the heaters, adequate electric lighting is also needed to.facilitate examination of bonsai at times convenient to the owner.

Money spent on a well-built shed is a wise investment, as spare bonsai pots, potting soils and other items may be stored in it, both in winter and during the summer months when the bonsai are outside. If the vertical planking and polystyrene are then removed and stored, a useful workbench area will be formed.

For those who do not have such a shed available, it is possible to over-winter bonsai in a specially-planned pit outside. The site should be carefully considered and if possible should be near the house and receive little sun, especially morning sun. A flat-bottomed pit of appropriate size, according to the number of trees you have, must be dug. As it will need covering, the simplest shape is rectangular, later extensions being to the length rather than the width. It will need a depth of at least 2 ft 6 in (75 cm), preferably greater, especially if the bonsai to be housed are large.

The bottom 6 in (15 cm) should then be filled with coarse chippings or similar material for drainage, this being covered in turn with a sheet of fine-grade plastic mesh to prevent the upper insulation materials, when they are added, from falling into the drainage material and choking it up. An inch (2.5 cm) of polystyrene is recommended for this (for its cleanness, lightness and ease of use), on which the bonsai are placed. The pots are then surrounded with more polystyrene chips which should also cover the pots. The pit must finally be covered and its success will depend on the degree of protection afforded by this covering. Cold frame lights are a useful starting point. These may be laid flat provided that a second sloping set of lights is erected above them to keep off rain and snow. Cover the flat lights with a thick, waterproof insulation. Polystyrene may again be used, or plastic sacks filled with shredded paper, straw or other such materials, flattened to form 2 to 3 in (5 to 8 cm) thick "blankets". Depending on predicted temperatures, two or more such layers may be used. The sloping cold frame lights are mounted above the "blankets" to protect them from the weather.

Bonsai kept in this manner are unlikely to require water more often than once a month when outside temperatures are below freezing, though they should, if possible, be checked more frequently.

APPENDIX B

IMPORTING PLANTS FROM ABROAD

It is currently very difficult to import bonsai into Britain from countries outside the EEC (European Economic Community). There is, however, a concession for passengers carrying up to five plants with their baggage. This applies as outlined below, the extracts having been taken from *Plant Health Import Legislation – Guide for Importers*, published by The Ministry of Agriculture, Fisheries and Food.

A total of up to five plants may be landed without a phytosanitary certificate, provided the material has been grown in the Euro-Mediterranean area and is imported with passenger baggage. This concession does *not* apply to the genera, *Malus, Prunus* or *Pyrus* or to the trees listed in Part 2.8. This list adds *Cydonia* to the list of banned trees, and in addition, no trees are permitted which are on the totally prohibited list. This comprises *Abies, Castanea, Larix, Picea, Pinus, Populus, Pseudotsuga, Quercus, Tsuga, Ulmus* and *Zelkova*.

As can be seen, this leaves very few species and permits nothing from Japan or the Far East (Japan is now classified as a prohibited area). Under licence (issued only to professional nurserymen) *Abies, Populus, Pseudotsuga, Ulmus* and *Zelkova* may be imported, provided they have fulfilled certain plant health requirements and are imported accompanied by the appropriate documents.

GLOSSARY OF
TECHNICAL TERMS

air-layer Technique used to make a new plant by inducing roots to form on a branch which has been wounded, with the wound being wrapped in sphagnum moss.

air-inarching Technique used to graft a branch into the trunk of a tree.

air root-grafting The grafting of roots on to a branch while this is still attached to a tree.

algae Aquatic or sub-aquatic plants varying from minute unicellular types to the large seaweeds. Those forming a green film on soil or other surfaces most concern the bonsai cultivator.

apex Top of tree.

apical bud A bud at the tip of a shoot.

axil The angle between the leaf stalk and the stem to which the former is attached.

Basho 17th century Japanese Haiku poet.

bud cuttings A bud with small piece of stem attached, used for propagation purposes.

bunjingi Literati style of bonsai with a long, slim, wandering trunk.

callus Tissue developed by woody plants over a wound.

candle Expanding new growth of pines.

candle flame style The shape, resembling a candle flame, into which *Ginkgo biloba* is normally trained.

capillary matting Man-made material capable of absorbing large amounts of water.

Chang Tse-Tsuan 11–12th century Chinese painter.

chichi Stalactite-like growth formed at the junction of a branch and trunk in aged specimens of *Ginkgo biloba*.

Chuwatari Pots made in China in the early 1900s for the Japanese market.

chokkan A single trunk standing upright on a single root.

cloud foot The ornate, sloping foot of certain pots.

cold-frame An unheated structure for protecting plants in winter against the worst of the weather, having a removable glass light (or lights).

cone The fruit of a conifer.

conifer Trees, usually evergreen, with needle-like or linear leaves, cone-bearing.

cool greenhouse One in which the temperature does not drop below $40°F$ ($4.5°C$).

coral spot (*Nectria cinnabarina*) A fungus common on dead twigs and branches which may infect living branches through wounds.

crown The uppermost part of a tree.

crown gall (*Bacterium tumefaciens*) Irregular swellings found on plant roots caused by a wound parasite.

cuttings *Softwood*: immature shoots used for propagation. *Semi-hardwood*: partially mature shoots used for propagation; and *Hardwood*: mature shoots used for propagation.

cultivar A garden variety of a plant, readily identifiable by certain characteristics, which it retains when reproduced from seed or vegetatively.

damping-off An attack by a parasitic fungus on seedlings, causing them to collapse.

deciduous A tree or shrub that loses its leaves at the end of the growing season.

defoliate Total leaf removal, used with bonsai to induce the growth of smaller leaves.

dormancy Resting period of plants when little or no growth is made.

endemic Peculiar to a particular area.

ericaceous Belonging to the *Ericaceae* family.

etiolated Literally, whitened by lack of light, but used to describe long growths arising from the same cause.

evergreen Bearing foliage throughout the year.

eye-level In bonsai terms this means the ideal viewing level for a bonsai. Eye-level should be two-thirds of the way up the trunk.

family A major grouping of plants, invariably comprising more than one genus and often a great many genera.

fukinagashi A slanting bonsai tree in which most of the branches are swept in one direction as if blown by the wind.

fukuroshiki-bachi Pots with incurved lips.

fungicide A substance for killing fungal diseases.

genetic make-up Hereditary resemblances due to interaction of genes.

genus A group of plants having distinctive structural characteristics in common.

germination The first stage in the growth of a plant from seed.

gyaku-bosori-eda A branch growing out, then back towards the trunk.

Hachi-no-ki A famous play, *Trees in Pots*, by Seami (1363-1444).

haiku A form of Japanese poetry.

half-hardy Trees and plants which need some form of winter protection.

han-en-eda A faulty branch in bonsai terms with a silhouette like a semi-circle.

han kengai A semi-cascade bonsai, in which the main trunk comes below the edge of the pot.

heel of cutting The expanded base of a side shoot after pulling it away from the main stem of a plant.

hiji-tsuki-eda An elbow-shaped branch – faulty in bonsai terms.

hokidachi Broom style, i.e. a single trunk with its branches uniformly fanned.

horai A style of training of Japanese white pine (*Pinus parviflora*).

humidity The level of water vapour in the atmosphere.

Ibei-ito A noted nurseryman and author of the early 18th century.

ikada Raft style, i.e. a single tree laid on its side with its branches grown as trunks.

indole-3-acetic acid A plant hormone inhibiting lateral bud development; also used in rooting of cuttings.

ipometsuki-eda Eye-poking, i.e. a forward-pointing branch of a bonsai, below eye-level.

ishitsuki A tree with exposed roots grasping a rock and growing over it before they enter the soil in the container.

jack Japanese tool for bending trunks and branches.

jin A branch stripped of its bark for artistic effect.

jinning tool A pliers-like tool for creating jin.

kabudachi A tree with three or more trunks growing from a single root.

Kamakura The period 1180–1333.

kannuki-eda A branch exactly opposite to and level with another, considered a fault in bonsai.

karami-eda Entangled branches, another fault in bonsai cultivation.

Kasugagongen-genki Picture scroll by Takakane Takashina – 1309.

Kataokaware Japanese pots of quality in natural shades.

kengai A tree, the main trunk of which descends below the bottom of the pot.

kengai-giku Cascade-trained chrysanthemum.

Kobeware A type of Japanese pot in unglazed dark brown.

kowatari Antique Chinese pots.

kuruma-eda Branches radiating from a trunk like the spokes of a wheel – a fault in bonsai cultivation.

Lao Tsu Chinese author, 6th century BC, of *Tao Te Ching*.

lateral Side shoots arising from a stem or branch.

leader Main stem.

leaf-mould Partially decayed dead leaves.

Lingnan A school of bonsai training initiated by Cantonese growers at the beginning of the 20th century.

Li Shih-Hsing Chinese painter of Yuan dynasty (AD1250–1368).

loam A fertile soil of good consistency which, at its most desirable for potting purposes, is from pasture-land.

mame Miniature bonsai.

micro-climate Localised climatic conditions that prevail in the immediate vicinity of a plant.

miki-kiri-eda A branch crossing a trunk – a fault in bonsai terms.

mineral salts Salts of minerals in the soil necessary for plant growth.

mist propagation equipment Equipment which produces a fine, intermittent mist spray to aid the rooting of cuttings.

moyogi Informal upright style.

Muro-machi Period following Kamakura – 1333–1603.

nadekaku A rectangular, straight-sided pot with rounded corners.

Nanga The cultural movement followed by painters of the Southern School of Chinese landscape painting.

node The point on a stem from which leaves spring.

parthenogenesis Method of asexual reproduction.

photosynthesis The manufacture of food substances by leaves, using carbon dioxide, water and sunlight.

pinch out To remove shoots or foliage with the fingers.

pinnate A leaf which consists of several leaflets, oppositely arranged in pairs, on a common stalk.

propagating frame Glass or plastic frame in which plants are propagated, with or without heat.

pruning The removal of leaves, shoots, twigs or branches, usually to stimulate new growths or improve the balance or health (by removing dead or weak wood) of a tree or shrub.

pyrethrum An insecticide prepared from the dried flower-heads of *Chrysanthemum cinerariifoliom* and *C. roseum*.

raceme An elongated inflorescence with stalked flowers arising from a central stem.

respiration The emission of carbon dioxide by plants during the hours of darkness.

root pruning The removal of roots (or parts of roots), used in dwarfing bonsai.

sabamiki A bark-stripping technique.

sagari-eda A dangling branch, considered a fault in bonsai.

seedling Young plant after germination.

sensei Teacher.

shakan A slanting or leaning trunk.

shidare-zukuri An upright tree with weeping branch style.

shinkire-eda A stubby branch, a fault in bonsai.

shinnashi A tree without an apex, a fault in bonsai.

shinwatari Pots made in China in the early 1900s for the Japanese market.

sidebranch cutters A kind of Japanese branch-pruning tool.

sokan A trunk divided in two, arising from a single root.

species Subordinate in classification to genus, differing only from the former in matters of detail.

sphagnum moss A type of moss which grows in bogs and swamps. Used as bonsai packing material and has the ability to retain water.

stratification The practice of over-wintering seeds of hardy plants either out of doors or by using a refrigerator to break dormancy and induce germination.

sucker A shoot springing from a subterranean stem or root of a plant.

suiban A shallow Japanese plant tray without drainage holes in the base.

sumiire Rectangular pot having a lip with the corners cut off.

tachi-eda An upward-growing branch, considered a fault in bonsai terms.

taikodo A round pot, "tyre-shaped".

Takakane Takashina 14th century Japanese artist.

tako A coiled trunk style of training bonsai which has been superceded by horai (which see).

Tao An ancient Chinese philosophy, literally "The Way".

Tao Te Ching A 6th-century Chinese philosophical work written by Lao Tsu.

Tap-root The main root of a tree, which acts as an anchor.

training pot A shallow pottery container used for training bonsai.

transpiration A continuing natural water loss from leaf and stem surfaces.

tray A very shallow bonsai container.

trunk cracker A pincer-like tool used to split trunks.

turntable A round, rotating platform to facilitate the rotation of a tree while training branches.

uchien Rectangular incurved pots with rounded corners.

uro An artistic, artificially produced trunk cavity where a large branch has been removed.

variegation Contrasting colour patterns on a leaf.

variety A sub-division of species, with plants holding this rank displaying variations from the parent. It relates only to plants from the wild.

vestigial bud An imperfectly developed bud.

viability The capacity of seeds to germinate.

whorl An arrangement of leaves or flowers resembling the spokes of a wheel.

wiring The technique of winding wire round a branch, stem or trunk to change its shape.

Yamaki High-quality Japanese pots, ranging in colour from sandy brown to gunmetal and silvery-grey.

yose-ue Several trees planted together in a single pot, giving the appearance of a forest or grove.

Zen Regarded as a religion by its followers although without sacred scriptures, fixed canon, rigid dogma, Saviour or divine being. It aims to bring about a high degree of self-knowledge.

INDEX

Page numbers in *italics* refer to illustrations

NORTHERN HEMISPHERE CLIMATIC CHART

		LONDON U.K.	COLOGNE W. GERMANY	DELHI INDIA	MIAMI U.S.A	NEW YORK U.S.A.
JAN	Temp.	39°F – 4°C	36°F – 2.5°C	57°F – 14°C	67°F – 19.5°C	30°F – -1°C
	Rainfall	2.0in – 51mm	2.0in – 51mm	0.9in – 23mm	2.8in – 71mm	3.7in – 9.7cm
FEB	Temp.	40°F – 4.5°C	38°F – 3.5°C	62°F – 17°C	68°F – 20°C	31°F – 0.5°C
	Rainfall	1.5in – 38mm	1.8in – 46mm	0.7in – 18mm	2.1in – 54mm	3.8in – 9.6cm
MAR	Temp.	44°F – 7°C	43°F – 6°C	72°F – 22.5°C	71°F – 22°C	37°F – 3°C
	Rainfall	1.4in – 36mm	1.8in – 46mm	0.5in – 12.7mm	2.5in – 63mm	3.6in – 9.2cm
APR	Temp.	48°F – 9°C	49°F – 9.5°C	82°F – 28°C	73°F – 23°C	49°F – 9.5°C
	Rainfall	1.8in – 46mm	1.9in – 48mm	0.3in – 7.6mm	3.2in – 8.1cm	3.2in – 8.1cm
MAY	Temp.	54°F – 12.5°C	57°F – 14°C	92°F – 33.5°C	77°F – 25°C	60°F – 16°C
	Rainfall	1.8in – 46mm	2.0in – 52mm	0.5in – 12mm	6.8in – 17.5cm	3.2in – 8cm
JUN	Temp.	60°F – 16°C	62°F – 17°C	92°F – 33.5°C	80°F – 27°C	68°F – 20°C
	Rainfall	1.6in – 40.5mm	2.6in – 66mm	2.9in – 71mm	7.0in – 18cm	3.3in – 84mm
JUL	Temp.	64°F – 18°C	65°F – 18.5°C	88°F – 31°C	82°F – 28°C	74°F – 23.5°C
	Rainfall	2.0in – 51mm	3.2in – 8.1cm	7.1in – 18.5cm	6.1in – 15.5cm	4.2in – 10.5cm
AUG	Temp.	63°F – 17.5°C	64°F – 18°C	86°F – 30°C	82°F – 28°C	73°F – 23°C
	Rainfall	2.2in – 56mm	2.8in – 71mm	6.8in – 17.5cm	6.3in – 16cm	4.3in – 11cm
SEP	Temp.	59°F – 15°C	59°F – 15°C	84°F – 29°C	81°F – 27.5°C	69°F – 29.5°C
	Rainfall	1.8in – 46mm	2.1in – 54mm	4.6in – 12cm	8.0in – 20cm	3.4in – 8.6cm
OCT	Temp.	51°F – 10.5°C	51°F – 10.5°C	79°F – 26.5°C	77°F – 25°C	59°F – 15°C
	Rainfall	2.3in – 58mm	2.5in – 64mm	0.4in – 10mm	9.2in – 23.5cm	3.5in – 9cm
NOV	Temp.	44°F – 7°C	43°F – 6°C	68°F – 20°C	72°F – 22.5°C	44°F – 7°C
	Rainfall	2.5in – 63mm	2.2in – 56mm	0.1in – 2.7mm	2.8in – 71mm	3.0in – 8cm
DEC	Temp.	40°F – 4.5°C	38°F – 3.5°C	59.5°F – 15°C	69°F – 20.5°C	35°F – 2°C
	Rainfall	2.0in – 52mm	2.5in – 64mm	0.4in – 10mm	2.0in – 51mm	3.6in – 9.2cm

Note: It may be necessary to make adjustments for local conditions which vary from those of the average for a whole country.